SCREEN PRINTING AT HOME

SCREEN PRINTING AT HOME

KAREN LEWIS

PRINT YOUR OWN FABRIC
TO MAKE SIMPLE SEWN PROJECTS

D&C
David and Charles

CONTENTS

INTRODUCTION

Be warned, screen printing is utterly addictive! About three years ago I took a short course at my local college – two hours a week for five weeks – and I haven't looked back since. From the first minute on the first day I was hooked, and the 8,640 minutes before the next lesson dragged for what felt like an eternity! I just couldn't wait to get back to the studio.

Ever since I was little I have been addicted to fabric, sewing and making, thanks to my Grandma. She had her machine and fabrics out constantly and I used to love delving through the beautiful treasure while she created on her old Singer. A lot later when my love of sewing was rekindled – after it had been pushed aside for sport, boys, good times, husband and babies – I discovered stunning screen printed fabrics from artists not only in the UK but also in Australia, the USA, South Africa and other far flung places. My creating was now taking place in the internet era, a time when it was possible to source all that wonderful talent from my kitchen table. I was in heaven, and whilst I was in love with sewing these beautifully creative, immensely tactile fabrics, I knew deep down I wanted to be sewing with my own created fabrics.

It was a while again later – once work, children and family commitments had subsided – before I had the opportunity of trying it for myself. But boy, when I did, something exploded in me and I haven't been the same since!

Screen printing is the art of transferring your own images, whether they be simple doodles or more intricate repeat designs, onto a material, such as paper, fabric or ceramic. It is incredibly versatile and

personal. There is something immensely satisfying about seeing the design that you sat and doodled being transferred to a screen, followed by the physical process of actually printing it onto your chosen surface. Screen printing allows you to print not one, but multiples of the same design, each one coming out slightly different, which to me is the delight of hand-printed fabric rather than a factory printed roll.

The versatility of hand printed fabric is enormous, from printing one-off silhouettes for a cushion or printing a repeated pattern, to using it in quilting or a number of other sewing projects. It has the mystery of being an incredibly technical process where surely you have to enrol in a college degree with high-tech facilities in order to come anywhere close to success. It certainly can be that complicated, but it can also be the simplest technique ever, where you can make beautiful objects literally from your kitchen table.

This book aims to teach you the simple basic steps of screen printing, from the equipment you need, to step by step instructions of different ways to prepare your screen, with simple projects to create with your beautiful, unique fabric.

I hope you will be as enthusiastic as I am as you work through the process and take delight in creating your own designs. I do apologize now though, as the world around you will change when you start printing. Everything will become an inspiration to you – from the shadows the trees make, to the simple patterns of the lines in the road. The world around you will never be the same again!

HOW TO USE THIS BOOK

This book aims to show how you can learn to screen print onto fabric sitting at your kitchen table. Whilst you can screen print onto any surface, we're going to look specifically at how to screen print onto fabric.

I will describe the minimum equipment and space that you need to start, several easy-to-do, at-home methods of preparing a screen, and how best to achieve prints from whichever method you choose. All the screen preparation methods in this book use simple and readily available equipment to enable you to successfully print at home with great results.

The clear step by step instructions, from what equipment and space you need, preparing your screen and printing, right through to making your fabric suitable for use in the sewing projects, will be covered here. The projects include a short 'no sew' section, with ideas of items you can print directly onto, ready to use as soon as the ink dries. Then the sewing projects give clear design and sewing templates to use to make the item – please do feel free to be adventurous and mix them around or use your own prints.

All the necessary templates for the projects can be found in the Design Templates and Sewing Templates sections, as can a list of suppliers from which to source the necessary equipment. Almost everything you need for printing and sewing can be found from a good local art or craft store, or from the online stores listed.

WORKING SPACE

One of the most important considerations in deciding where to print is the space you have around your printing area. Not only do you need a space large enough for your screen, but you also need room to move around it, a drying area for your printed fabric, and a place to rest your screen between prints.

You don't want to rest your screen flat between prints as the paint on the underside will mark your printing area. Instead, attach your screen to hinge clamps and keep your screen raised, or alternatively you could use a wooden baton to rest the screen on.

You need to have plenty of room to keep your area clean and also plenty of space to move your printed items to, whether it be table space, a drying rack or perhaps constructing a temporary line to peg your fabrics from.

As well as deciding where to print, you also need an area to clean your screen. Ideally this would be outside with a hose. You can clean your screen in a large sink or bath, but be mindful that if you are printing regularly the paint can clog the sink (see Finishing Up).

ESSENTIAL PRINTING MATERIALS

We will go on to discuss the different methods of preparing a screen and what you need for this later in the book, but whatever method you choose, you will need the following basic equipment:

1. SCREEN PRINTING FRAME

I would always suggest choosing an aluminium frame, as this dries much quicker after cleaning than a wooden frame, and it can be wiped down so you can use it again sooner. They are a little more expensive than wooden screens but wood can be prone to warping, so aluminium is a better investment.

Always choose a frame as big as your space allows. You don't need to use the entire size of your screen for every design, but this does give you the flexibility of making bigger prints if you want.

Maybe you only have a tiny space to print and no suitable area to wash up? A fantastic method suitable for any space is to use an embroidery hoop with muslin (cheesecloth) fabric stretched tightly across instead of

EQUIPMENT

Printing screen (1)/ Mesh (2) / Squeegee (3) / Inks (4) / Parcel tape (5) Spatulas (6) / Towels (7) / Fabric paint/Inks mixed with textile medium (8)

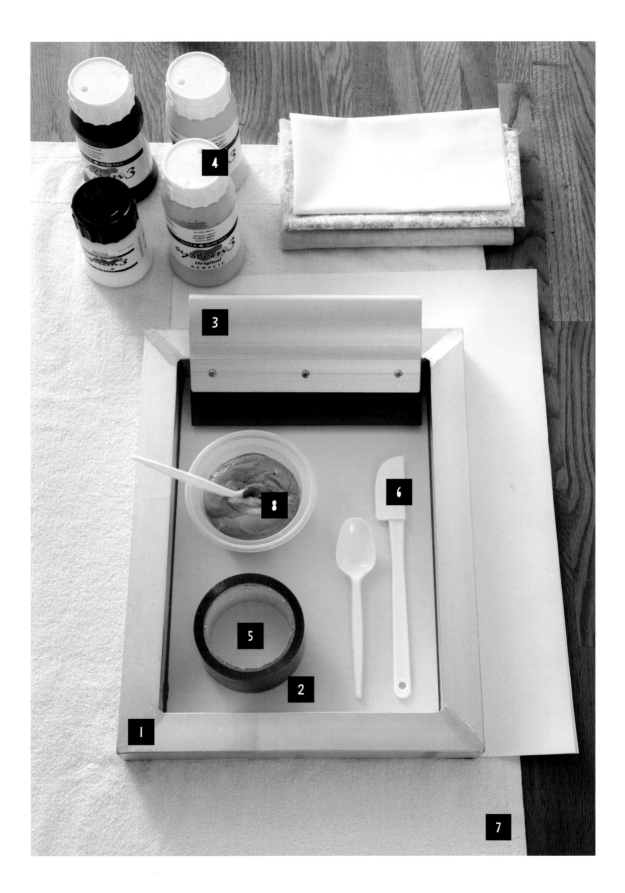

a fully sized screen (9). You will be limited to the size of your design but it is perfectly possible to produce a fantastic screen print with this method. Using an old credit card or similar to act as a squeegee, simply pull the paint across the muslin (10). You don't even need to wash anything out when you have finished; simply unfasten your hoop and throw everything away, just wiping down and saving the hoop for next time!

2. MESH

Mesh is the woven fabric that is pulled tightly across the screen printing frame, and frames can be bought with this mesh in place. Historically, this was made from silk, hence the name silk-screen printing. Nowadays, the mesh is generally made of polyester.

Mesh comes in a variety of thread counts, a little like bed linen, which describes how many strands per inch are in the mesh fabric. A lower mesh count has fewer strands and therefore wider spaces between them. The ink flows through the screen more easily with a lower mesh count, so this is generally used for less detailed artwork and printing onto rougher or more textured surfaces like fabric. A higher mesh count has less space for the ink to flow through, so is generally used for more detailed artwork and smoother surfaces. For printing onto fabric I would recommend a mesh count of about 110; as a beginner you will find this is more than adequate for different textured fabrics that you may use. If you find your designs are very detailed you may want to try a higher count.

Mesh comes in either white

or yellow; personally I would always opt for yellow. Yellow mesh absorbs more light and when you are cleaning or reclaiming your screen you want to be able to hold it up to the light and check that you have removed all the paint from it.

3. SQUEEGEE

A screen printing squeegee is a very firm rubber blade that is attached to either a metal or wooden handle. Again, I would opt for investing in an aluminium one for the same reasons as an aluminium screen. The size of the squeegee is very important. You need it to pull across the width of your design with a little overlap to ensure a clean print, as well as being a couple of inches narrower than the width of your screen to allow for the ink to be pushed outwards as you print.

4. INKS

You can use water-based acrylic inks or oil-based Plastinol inks; like anything it is down to personal preference. I like to use water-based acrylic inks as they have a softer finish and sink into the fabric, unlike Plastinol ink that sits on top of the fabric, giving the print a raised, plastic texture.

If you are using water-based acrylic ink, you will need to mix this with a textile medium to make the paint permanent when heat setting with an iron (see How to Print – Preparing your Inks). You can, however, buy some ready-mixed fabric paints. The advantage of these is you don't need to spend a lot of money to get started, but you may find colour choices are more limited.

5. PARCEL TAPE

You will need to tape around the inside of the frame with parcel tape to prevent paint from leaking through where the mesh meets the frame. Once this has been done you can keep the same tape on your screen until it needs to be replaced.

6. SPATULAS

At the end of your printing session you will want to scoop up any remaining ink back into the pot for next time; the ink hasn't got dirty and is perfectly suitable to use again. You just need to have a plastic spatula or scraper to hand to scoop up any excess ink.

7. TOWELS

Printing on fabric can be tricky, with the fabric being prone to sliding on your work surface. To prevent this from happening, lay an old towel or blanket down and sit your screen on top. You will find this is all the extra friction you need to keep everything in place.

A polyester mesh is pulled tightly across the screen printing frame, as shown. Ensure your frame is as big as your space allows.

CHOOSING YOUR TECHNIQUE

There are three main methods to prepare your screen with your design in order to screen print. The simplest and quickest is designing and cutting a paper stencil. The second is using drawing fluid and screen filler, and the third is using photo emulsion to expose your screen. The first two methods can easily be done at home and it is these two methods that we are going to learn about in this book, so you can screen print with confidence.

Stencil printing is perfect for simple designs and silhouettes that lend themselves to a block colour with minimal detail to cut out. You can be quite adventurous with paper cutting, and there are some amazing examples of paper cutting artists in the industry today. But since this is a temporary method

that you can only print from in one sitting, it seems a shame to go to the trouble of being very intricate in your cutting only to have to throw the stencil away at the end of your printing session. If you want a lot more detail in your design you are best working with the screen filler method. There are, however, ways of using stencils in a more permanent way by cutting them from acetate paper or a print and cut film. These materials are quite expensive so you may want to try your design out with newsprint paper first.

The screen filler method takes a little longer to prepare but it does allow you to produce a more detailed image, and is also a more permanent method. If you want to keep a design on your screen to use again, this is a better choice.

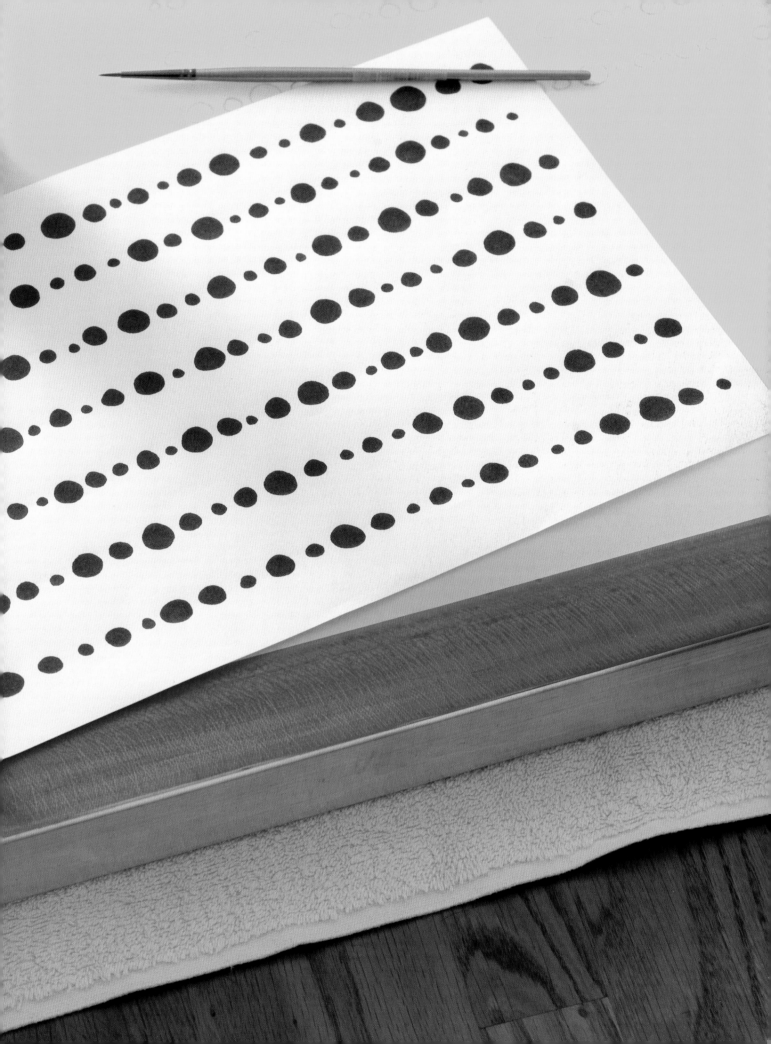

STENCIL TECHNIQUE

You will be cutting stencils out of newsprint paper with a craft knife. Make sure your paper is at least

the size of the outer dimension of your frame, as you can always cut it down to size later if it is a little

big. Newsprint paper is the perfect paper for stencils as it is very thin and therefore sits flush onto the

mesh without creating a thick edge where paint can sit too thickly and blur as you lift up the screen. As

well as being thin it is also absorbent, which makes it stick to the mesh as the paint is pulled through.

EQUIPMENT

The basic equipment you need for this technique is as follows:
Cutting mat (1)/ Newsprint paper (2) / Parcel tape (3) / Masking tape
(4) / Ruler (5) / Pencil (6) / Craft knife (7) / Fingertip craft knife (8)

CREATING A CUT-OUT STENCIL

1. Decide on the image you want to screen print. When selecting an image you need to think about the size of the frame that you are using. Leave about 7½cm (3in) of space at the top and bottom of the frame and 5cm (2in) at the sides. This will mean that when you are printing, the ink is pulled clear across the design and doesn't rest on the open gaps of the mesh between prints. This can cause excess ink to flood through and ruin your print. Once you have checked the size, draw or print your design (A).

2. Resting on a cutting mat to protect your table, carefully cut out your design using a craft knife (B). Remember that what you are cutting out is where the paint will be, and this is the pattern you will see.

3. When you have finished cutting out your design hold it up to the light, or place it on top of a solid dark surface to check you have cut away all the bits that you need to get a clear print of your design. Once you are happy you can attach it to your screen.

4. Attach the stencil to the underside of the frame (the side where the frame is flush with the mesh) remembering to reverse your image if necessary. Using masking tape, tape the paper on all four sides, making sure it is pulled flat with no creases (C). Check at this point that the image is central to your frame and there is room all around your cut design for the ink to be pulled clear of it.

MORE WAYS TO CREATE A STENCIL

Using a paper stencil to produce an image for screen printing is a very flexible method and can be done in many unique ways. As well as producing a cut out stencil, think of other ways you can block ink onto the mesh to produce a design. Experiment and have fun! The only advice I would give you is to practice on newsprint paper rather than on expensive fabric. If the idea works then go onto printing on your fabric.

Cut out shapes and use these to block out the ink and print around the shapes.

Use a low tack masking tape – washi tape is good – to make shapes directly on your screen.

Doilies are fantastic to use as stencils. Tape over any area next to the doily where you don't want ink to come through.

Hopefully you can see that there are many ways to create a stencil.

SCREEN FILLER TECHNIQUE

Using drawing fluid and screen filler is an excellent technique to start introducing further detail into your work. The drawing fluid essentially blocks any applied screen filler, which means that wherever you paint drawing fluid will be where paint comes through the screen filler to create your design as you print.

Have a play around to become used to the process before you begin. Once you begin using the drawing fluid you can always wash away any mistakes, but you will need to wait for the mesh to dry before continuing.

I also suggest that you practise painting drawing fluid onto paper first to achieve a finish you really like.

In addition, if you apply one coat of drawing fluid to the mesh you will see the brushstrokes, whereas applying several coats will result in a more solid print. Preparing your screen using this technique takes a while, so ensure you do this the day before you are planning to actually print.

EQUIPMENT

The basic equipment you need for this technique is as follows: Printing screen (1) / Squeegee (2) / Screen filler (3) / Drawing fluid (4) / Spatulas (5) / Masking tape (6) / Soft B pencil (7) /

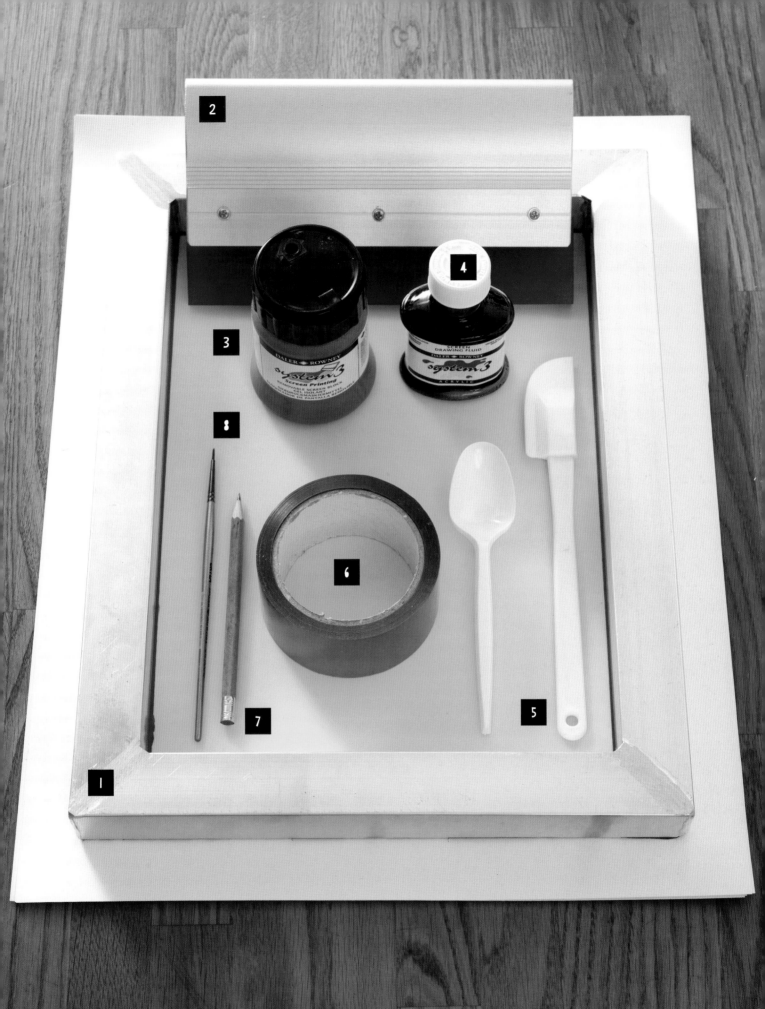

CREATING A SCREEN FILLER

1. Choose the image you wish to use and trace this with pencil onto your screen, with the mesh side facing down. Ensure you use a soft B pencil so that it marks the mesh easily and isn't so sharp that you risk tearing the mesh. Apply light pencil marks to start with; if you can't see the pencil lines from the other side of the screen you will need to use an even softer lead. The pencil lines will be guides for the drawing fluid, so it is vital you can see them from the other side of the screen (A).

2. Turn your screen over and start using your brush to apply drawing fluid to your pencil lines, which should be visible (B). As you work, apply the drawing fluid as carefully and accurately as you can – this will be the exact design that will be printed. However don't worry if your work isn't perfect; imperfections are characterful and you want to create the impression of hand-drawn work, rather than a computer printout.

3. When you have finished painting on the design, allow the drawing fluid to dry completely, keeping your mesh flat to avoid any drips (C). This could take all night, but you can speed up the process by placing the mesh next to a radiator, or even use a hairdryer; in the latter case the drying process may not take much more than an hour or two. The drawing fluid is completely dry when it is no longer tacky to the touch. Be patient at this stage and don't be tempted to move onto the next step until there is no tackiness at all; the screen filler may not adhere properly if applied too early.

4. Now mix the jar of screen filler thoroughly and use a spatula to spoon it onto the mesh at the top of the screen, above the design so you have plenty of room to pull it past smoothly (D). Pour on a line of screen filler measuring about 2½cm (1in) in width, as shown. It's fine to pour

on more than you need, as you can spoon any excess back into the jar to use next time; however, you want to avoid too much mess, so try to pour on about the right amount.

5. Take a squeegee with a length just short of the mesh width and hold it towards you at an angle of about 45 degrees, as shown (E). Then gently but firmly use it to pull down the screen filler in a single motion, coating the mesh.

6. You will probably need to leave your prepared screen to dry overnight. As with the drawing fluid, you can speed up the process by leaving it by a radiator or by using a hairdryer. Don't be tempted to move onto the next step until the screen filler is completely dry (F) – it may seem dry on top, but if it isn't dry all the way through it will rub away as you wash the screen. It is definitely better to be safe than sorry where this is concerned.

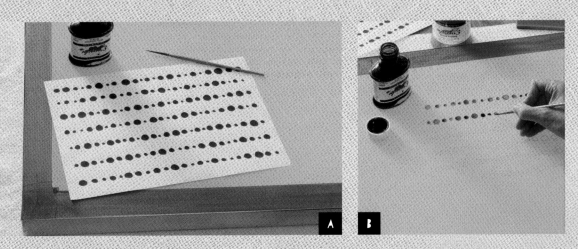

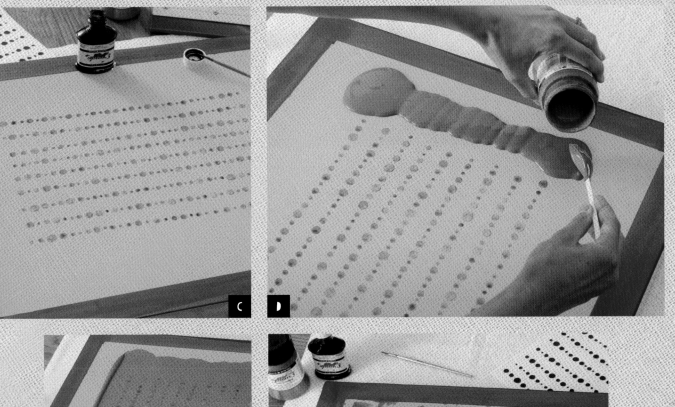

HOW TO PRINT

Now that you have prepared your screen, let's get ready to print! The printing method is the same whether you are using the screen filler or the stencil method. Screen printing is a technique that you will perfect as you practise, so please don't give up if your first attempts do not come out how you imagined; it is a skill that improves with experience. If you are struggling, use the Troubleshooting section to identify what is going wrong. A great tip is to write on any imperfect prints what you think went wrong then keep these as your own learning resource. We all learn from our mistakes and believe me, you will make some!

I suggest you practise on newsprint paper rather than your precious fabric. Newsprint is obviously a lot cheaper than fabric and you want to be able to practise freely without worrying about how much fabric you are going through. There will come a time when you need to perfect your printing skills on fabric, but hopefully by then your general technique will have become a lot more consistent.

BE PREPARED

PREPARING THE WORKSPACE

One of the most important things with screen printing is to be prepared. Once you start printing, you need to work relatively quickly and continuously, otherwise the ink in your screen can start to dry and clog up the mesh. It is pretty tricky to unclog it and the only thing you can do is wash out your screen, wait for it to dry and start again. You can help to avoid doing this by having everything ready and to hand.

Make sure you have all the equipment that you need in your printing space. Amongst other things, have your inks to hand already mixed, an old towel for you to lean on, spare newsprint paper, your fabric ironed and cut to size, scrapers, and kitchen paper (paper towel) for blotting unwanted splashes and spillages. Even keep a little paintbrush to hand so you can carefully stipple any gaps that need filling in.

The final thing you need is an old towel or blanket that you don't mind getting paint on to place under your screen. Fabric can have a tendency to slip if it is positioned directly on a smooth worktop, so to avoid this from happening you need to rest your screen on a non slippery surface. This allows the screen to sit on top of the fabric without it sliding about and makes printing much easier.

With the question of being prepared comes the question of where to print. Is the space you have chosen big enough to spread everything out without the worry of getting paint everywhere? You need to be able to move your screen around between prints, as you change your paper and fabric from print to print.

Another consideration of where to print is the space you need to dry your prints. Maybe you are lucky enough to have a large table to lay all your prints out on as you work. Or maybe you have room to put a clothes dryer next to where you are working. If not, you can always construct a temporary washing line and peg your prints up as you go. Don't be tempted to dry your prints outside, however warm, as any gusts of wind could blow bits onto your not quite dry fabric, as well as folding the fabric in on itself so the paint rubs.

Ensure you have all the equipment you need at your workspace, including inks, your printing frame, an old towel to lean on, as well as somewhere to dry your prints such as a clothes dryer.

PREPARING YOUR INKS

If you are not using ready mixed fabric paints, and there are some good ready mixed varieties available, then you will need to mix your water-based acrylic paint with a textile medium to make it suitable for printing onto fabric. Use a wide necked jar or carton for this and mix the paint in the ratio of 1:1, with a slight leaning towards a little more medium to ink. Mix thoroughly until you can no longer see specks of the medium. Make sure your jar or carton has a lid, as this will prevent your paint from drying out between your printing sessions.

◄ You will need to mix your acrylic paint with a textile medium to make it suitable for printing onto fabric.

MAKING A PRINT

You are finally ready to print! You have prepared your screen; you have your paper, fabric, ink and frame rest at the ready. All that is left is to see the magic unfold and your design come to life as you take the steps of physically printing. Making a print is obviously the crucial step in the whole process so it is important that you are fully prepared with everything to hand. Do read through these steps before you start your printing, and practise on newsprint before attempting to print on expensive fabric, so you are completely clear about what you are going to do. Let's go!

1. Begin by placing a piece of newsprint under your screen. Pour plenty of ink along the top end of your screen (A); don't worry about waste, as any excess can be scooped up and put back into the pot.

2. Hold the screen with one hand (or get someone to hold it for you), and with your squeegee in your other hand, pull the ink across the screen in one smooth movement, with the squeegee at an angle of about 45 degrees (B). Make sure you bring the ink

past the end of your design to avoid it sitting in the open mesh and causing bleeding through the screen. Tap any excess ink off the squeegee and then, with it at the same angle, push the ink back up the screen.

3. Repeat this up and down action once more, but with the final push, lift the screen up off the paper at the near end and then push the ink up (C). This is called flooding the screen, which fills the mesh with ink and helps prevent it from drying out.

Move your screen to one side and rest it on a wooden baton or something similar, keeping the mesh off the surface to avoid paint shadows under the screen that will mark further prints. Move your printed piece to your drying area then move a clean piece of newsprint beneath the mesh to print again. Keep printing, moving onto fabric once you are confident with your technique. Repeat as many times as you want, but if your screen starts to dry up you will need to wash it immediately, letting it dry until the next time.

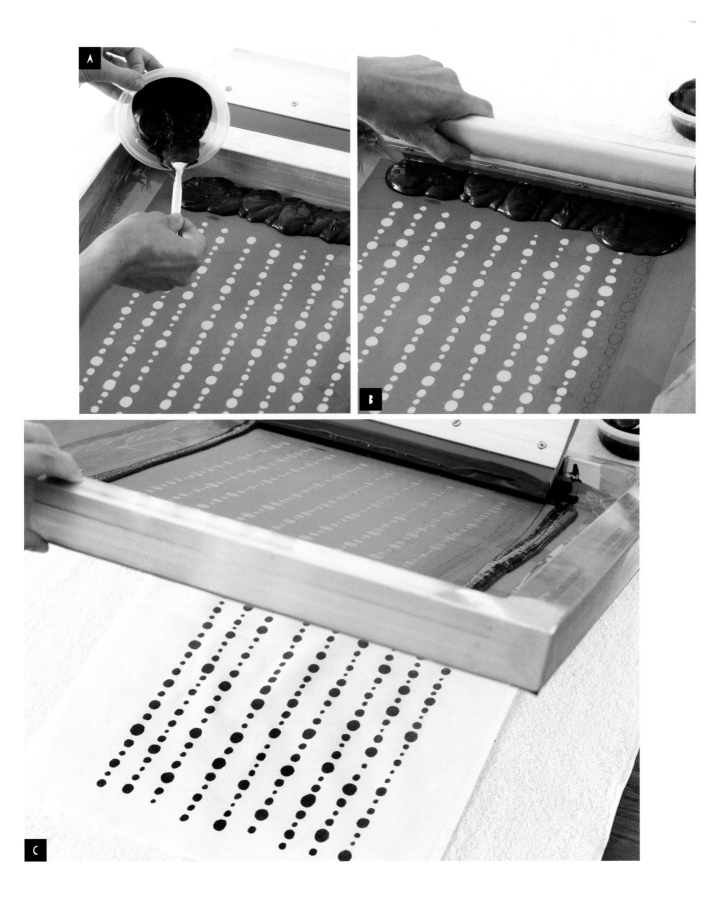

FINISHING UP

When you have finished printing, scoop any excess paint from your screen and put this back into your pot; it isn't dirty and you don't want to waste any by washing it away. Scrape as much off the screen as you can (you may be able to scrape a bit more from both sides when you have removed the stencil) and then wash your screen. You need to wash it straightaway after you have finished printing, as any dried paint can permanently clog it up, preventing paint from passing through next time you use it.

If you have printed using a stencil, peel it off, together with the tape, and throw it away. You will have to re-cut your design if you want to do it again. If you like the result of the design and think you will use it regularly, consider investing in some acetate sheets. These aren't the cheapest, but if you are going to print with the same stencil design regularly then they may be worth it.

Wash out the back of your screen first (the smooth side), hosing off as much of the paint as you can, then turn your screen around and hose down the rest, getting right into the corners. You want to restore your screen back to being as clean as possible every time to avoid any paint sticking in the mesh. If you used the screen filler method, it is harder to see if the screen is thoroughly cleaned. However, hold it up to natural light and you should be able to see through the mesh; if not, clean some more.

Leave your screen to dry off fully and then put it away, storing it standing up, so it is ready for the next time you use it.

▶ Thoroughly wash your screen as soon as you have finished printing to prevent dried paint from clogging it up.

36

TROUBLESHOOTING

Screen printing is a skill that can take a while to master and become natural. You will, without doubt, make mistakes with your printing, and it is useful to be able to assess what has happened so you can adjust for next time. Some accidents can be happy, but sometimes you will need to decide what needs correcting to get a cleaner print next time. With this in mind it is useful to write on any unsuccessful prints what you think went wrong to create a useful reference for improving your technique. Listed below are some common problems and what may have caused them.

PROBLEM	CAUSE
Too much ink passing through	Pulling the squeegee too many times, or with too much pressure, or too much medium mixed with paint
Not enough ink passing through	Pulling the squeegee too lightly, or not enough times, for the fabric texture or paint colour
Print not even on all sides	Pulling the squeegee with more pressure on one side than the other
Screen drying out	Taking too long between prints, or not enough ink on the screen, or not enough medium mixed with the paint
Flooding through screen in parts	Ink sitting on exposed mesh and not clearing the design when printing
Printed image blurring	Fabric or screen movement when printing
Design appearing in unwanted areas	Paint from the design has appeared on the underside of the screen due to the above

In most of these cases you will need to wash out your screen, front and back, let it dry and wait to start again. In the case of too much ink passing through, or excess ink being on the underside of the screen, you may be able to rectify this by making several lighter prints on newsprint to remove the excess before trying again. If this doesn't appear to be removing the excess ink in the mesh and under the screen, wash it out and start again. Once your screen has started drying out you will have to wash your screen immediately to avoid dried ink permanently clogging up the mesh.

Follow the instructions provided, and troubleshoot as needed, to improve your screen printing technique.

PRINTING ON FABRICS

Printing on fabric is an absolute delight and having your designs

available to sew in your projects is something you won't tire of.

There is endless scope to experiment on different types of fabrics,

too. However, printing on fabric, rather than on card or paper, can

bring its problems, as you will need to compensate for movement

in fabric and also for different textures.

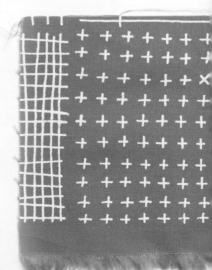

The easiest type of fabric to print on is one with a smooth texture and a close weave, like a quilting cotton, so I would suggest you try this first. It is more likely to be gripped by your screen, thus preventing movement. Also, due to its close weave and smooth finish, ink will be printed in a more even way.

A more open weave fabric has larger gaps where you can lose some of your design. If you want to eventually print on this kind of fabric, for instance open weave linen, choose a design with less detail, like a silhouette. This will give you a clearer print on this type of fabric. In the same way, a more textured fabric may not be great for more detailed printing, as some of the larger flecks may get in the way of the ink.

Try to avoid printing on very shiny, slippery fabric, like satin, as it is difficult to prevent these kinds of fabric from moving. However, it is not impossible, and one way is to

attach them to a board using either spray mount or masking tape, or by even using both.

Not only can you choose fabrics of varying textures, but you can also choose different coloured fabrics, and even plain or patterned. Printing on darker fabric needs more passings of the squeegee, as you will need a greater ink deposit in order for it to show up. Some colours of ink will show up better on different shades of fabric, but you can have fun experimenting with this.

Working with patterned fabric can create fantastic results. Checks are great for printing on and I am always keeping an eye out for my husband's old shirts to work on, waiting patiently for him to decide they are surplus to requirements! Vintage fabrics work really well too, and are great to use for all sorts of cushions, bags and other projects. Be on the lookout in charity shops for fabrics that you think would work well.

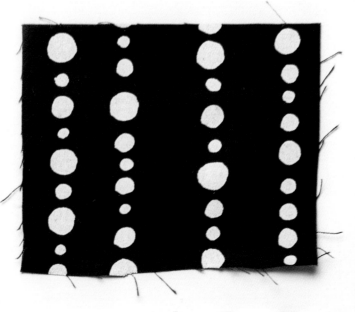

On these pages are shown some printed fabrics to give you an idea of what is possible. You will find some of the designs in the projects; I hope the others will inspire you to explore and create your own.

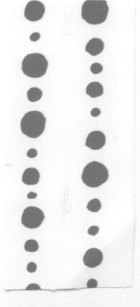

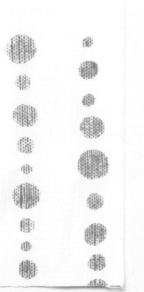

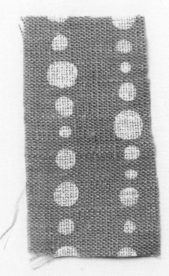

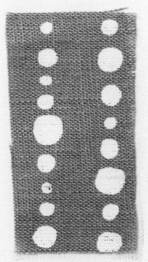

PREPARING YOUR FABRIC

Whatever fabric you choose to work with, you will need to prepare it for printing. Some fabrics have been covered with a starchy spray, which may have left a film on the fabric. You will need to wash your fabrics before you print to make sure you remove all of this coating.

After you have printed and the fabric is completely dry, you will need to heat set the fabric to make it washable. Resting it on parchment paper, iron on the reverse of the fabric for several minutes with a hot iron. Your fabric will now be suitable for washing on a cool wash. Whenever you wash your screen printed fabric, afterwards iron it again in the same way.

PROJECTS

There is so much creative potential in experimenting with different ways of preparing your screen to give different printing and design results, as well as different fabrics that you can use. All the following projects can be done using the designs and fabrics suggested, or you can experiment with your own ideas for them. Some designs may work better in some of the projects, but there are no rules here. Have fun trying out different things with different fabrics.

If you are using the designs and templates at the back of the book, they are all provided at actual size. Simply photocopy the required design and prepare your screen in the way outlined earlier in the book.

NO-SEW PROJECTS

I want to start you off with some no sew projects, so having just learnt screen printing techniques, you can quickly produce an item with your new skills without having to sew your printed fabric into something. Printing onto t-shirts, tea towels, tote bags, aprons and other readymade items is a wonderful way to experiment with your screen printing technique to produce instant results.

When screen printing onto tea towels that have a hanging tag already on them, make sure you are printing your design the right way round for the tag's position.

You will need to protect the back of t-shirts and tote bags when printing to prevent the paint sinking through, so always remember to put a piece of newsprint inside the layers. Keep this in position until your paint has dried.

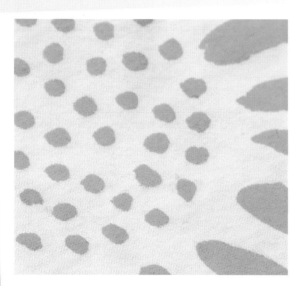

T-SHIRT

SCREEN FILLER TECHNIQUE

Printing on t-shirts is a fantastic way to bring instant originality to an ordinary item. You can experiment and have fun with all sorts of ideas for turning t-shirts into unique items of individual clothing. For this project I have used a happy sunflower design that would be perfect in a number of colours, and would work well on any t-shirt size – so make one for everyone you know while you are at it!

1. Using the Sunflower design, prepare your screen with the design, as described in the Screen Filler Technique section.

2. Place a protective piece of newsprint paper between the two layers of the t-shirt to prevent paint coming through, then print the sunflower onto the t-shirt. Leave to dry before heat setting.

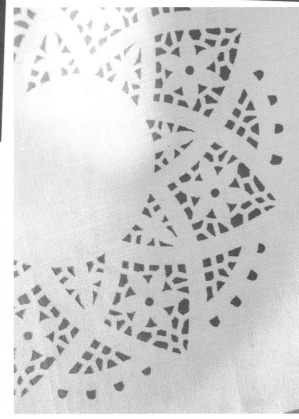

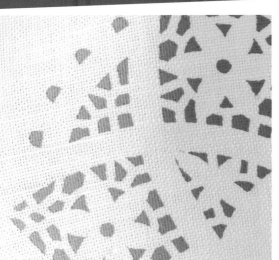

TEA TOWEL

STENCIL TECHNIQUE

Tea towels make wonderful items to screen print on – truly blank

canvases. They are perfect for printing a single large design;

alternatively, they look great with a repeated overall pattern. For

this project I have used a paper doily as a stencil on my screen.

When working on your own design, choose any size of doily

that fits well on your own screen, making sure enough space is

left between the doily and the frame to move the paint around.

I. Use a paper stencil
and attach it to your screen
as described in the Stencil
Technique section.

2. Print the doily design all
over your tea towel. Then leave
to dry before heat setting.

PILLOWCASE

STENCIL TECHNIQUE

Again, pillowcases make great blank canvases to which it is easy to add a touch of originality, and they work really well with a one-off print or a repeated overall design. For this project I have printed a cloud design using the embroidery hoop stencil method. Use the Cloud design to create your own dreamy pillow to rest your sleepy head.

1. Photocopy or trace the Cloud design onto newsprint paper.

2. Cut out the design with a craft knife and attach this to your embroidery hoop using the method described in Essential Printing Materials.

3. Place a protective piece of newsprint paper between the two layers of the pillowcase to prevent paint coming through. Then print the design all over your pillowcase using a credit card as a squeegee. Leave to dry before heat setting.

TOTE BAG

STENCIL TECHNIQUE

You can never have enough tote bags...well I can't! One for shopping, one for library trips and plenty more for storing things at home. This is a good item for trying out some design ideas. Using the stencil technique, cut out a stencil from the whimsical Giant Flower design to make a fun, colourful shopper that will bring a smile to your face when you are out and about.

1. Photocopy or trace the Giant Flower design onto newsprint paper. Cut this out and prepare your screen using this as your stencil.

2. Make sure your tote bag is the right way round before you start printing. Place a protective piece of newsprint paper between the two layers of the tote bag to prevent paint coming through then print the design. Leave to dry before heat setting.

SEWING PROJECTS

Now is the time to start combining your newly found screen printing skills with some sewing projects. No doubt by now you will have had fun seeing items come to life in the no sew section, and with the sewing projects provided here you will have the opportunity to sew your very own hand-printed fabric.

All the designs and colours suggested within each individual project are open to interpretation and, as already mentioned, you should have fun experimenting with different designs, colours, and fabrics. You could even try reducing or enlarging the design templates for different results.

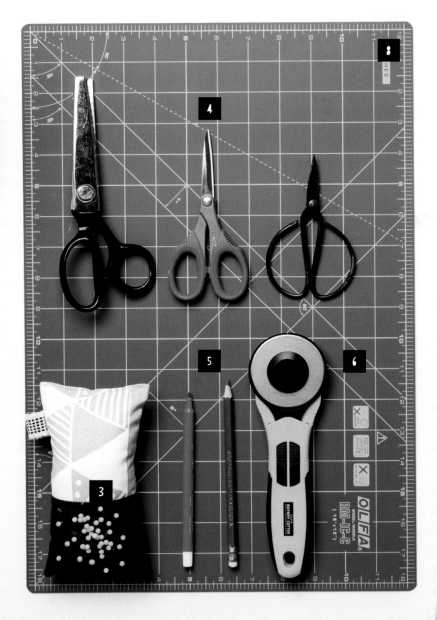

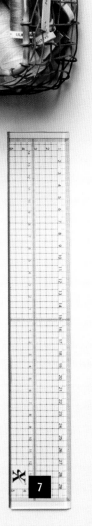

EQUIPMENT

For all of the following projects you will need:
Sewing machine (1) / Thread (2) / Pins (3) / Scissors (4)
Fabric pen/pencil (5) / Rotary cutter (6) / Ruler (7) / Cutting board (8)

TABLE RUNNER

SCREEN FILLER TECHNIQUE

A table runner is a lovely, casual way of bringing colour and texture into your home without hiding what is probably a delightful table underneath. I like to use a textured fabric such as linen, with a simple motif that adds interest but doesn't take over from everything else on the table. A table runner can be used to dress a table with a simple bunch of flowers picked from the garden, or used for a meal. Sometimes it is nice to have a short runner not quite reaching the ends of the table, and at other times one that hangs over the sides works well. All in all, a very versatile and simple project!

YOU WILL NEED:
★ Agapanthus design (see Agapanthus design)
★ Linen fabric, dimensions dependant on your table size, 5cm (2in) bigger than required size of runner
★ Pins
★ Sewing machine

1. Photocopy the Agapanthus design and prepare your screen using the screen filler method. Draw two lots of this design next to each other on your screen, thus creating six agapanthus in a row.

2. Decide where you would like the position of your design to be and print it carefully at both ends of your runner fabric. Allow to dry thoroughly and heat set.

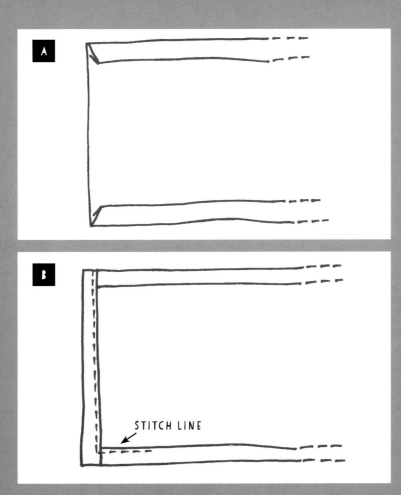

STITCH LINE

3. Fold and iron a 5mm (¼in) seam lengthways on both sides of your runner fabric. Repeat this so you have folded and pressed twice (A).

4. Repeat on both short ends of your runner so that all four edges have been folded and pressed twice.

5. Pin these four sides and then sew around just inside the fold line with a simple straight stitch or a more decorative stitch if you prefer (B).

6. Done! It was that simple, so now it's time to dress your table and put your feet up!

NAPKIN SET

SCREEN FILLER TECHNIQUE

Another simple project that is quick and easy to make, and is a great gift for anyone. I like linen for my table dressings so have used lovely, soft, textured linen to screen print a bubble design slightly off centre. You can position the design wherever you like on the napkins and vary it with each one. You could also try printing each napkin in a different colour, too.

YOU WILL NEED:
★ Bubbles design (see Bubbles design)
★ Linen fabric, 4 squares, each 5cm (2in) bigger all round than the required size
★ Pins
★ Sewing machine

1. Photocopy the Bubbles design and prepare your screen using the screen filler method.

2. Decide on the position of your design and print this carefully on all your fabrics. Allow to dry thoroughly and heat set by ironing on the reverse.

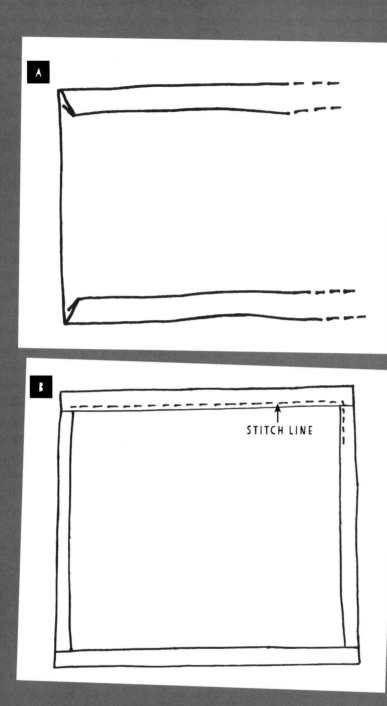

STITCH LINE

3. Fold and iron 5mm (¼in) seams on the top and bottom of the square fabric pieces and then the other two sides (A).

4. Repeat this so that all four edges have been folded and pressed twice.

5. Pin these four sides and then sew around just inside the fold line with a simple straight stitch or a more decorative stitch if you prefer (B).

6. Done! It was that simple, so it's time to sit down and have a little something to eat!

POT HOLDERS

STENCIL TECHNIQUE

I am very much a fan of the 19th Century textile designer William Morris, who once said "have nothing in your house that you do not know to be useful, or believe to be beautiful". There is nothing more appealing than prettying up day-to-day chores by using objects that are both useful and beautiful. These pot holders give a touch of colour and style hanging on a hook when not in use. I have added a strip of the screen printed Little Stem design on a neutral background and finished off with colourful binding and a tag. These pot holders are a great little project that instantly gives your kitchen a lift, and they make a great gift, too.

YOU WILL NEED:
★ Pot Holder template (see Sewing Templates)
★ Spray mount
★ Fabric pen
★ Pins
★ Sewing machine

FOR THE FRONT:
★ Little Leaf design (see Little Leaf design)
★ Printed panel fabric, 10 x 25cm (4 x 10in)
★ Coordinating fabric, 25 x 25cm
   (10 x 10in) cut into 2 pieces

FOR THE BACK:
★ Contrasting backing fabric, 25 x 25cm (10 x 10in)
★ Thick / insulated wadding (batting),
   25 x 25cm (10 x 10in)

FOR THE BINDING:
★ Binding fabric, 25 x 23cm (10 x 9in)

FOR THE HANGING TAG:
★ Binding fabric, 5 x 15cm (2 x 6in)

1. Photocopy or trace the Little Leaf design onto newsprint paper and cut out with a craft knife. Attach this to your screen and print one row onto your panel fabric. Allow to dry thoroughly and heat set.

2. To make the front of the pot holder, place the screen printed fabric and a piece of coordinating fabric, right sides facing, then pin down the long edge to secure and stitch in a straight line. Repeat to add the remaining coordinating piece on the opposite side of the screen printed fabric (A).

3. Sandwich together three layers of fabric: the front of your pot holder, the insulated wadding (batting) and the back. Do this by spray mounting the wadding and smoothly adding the front, then spray mount the back of the wadding and add the backing fabric.

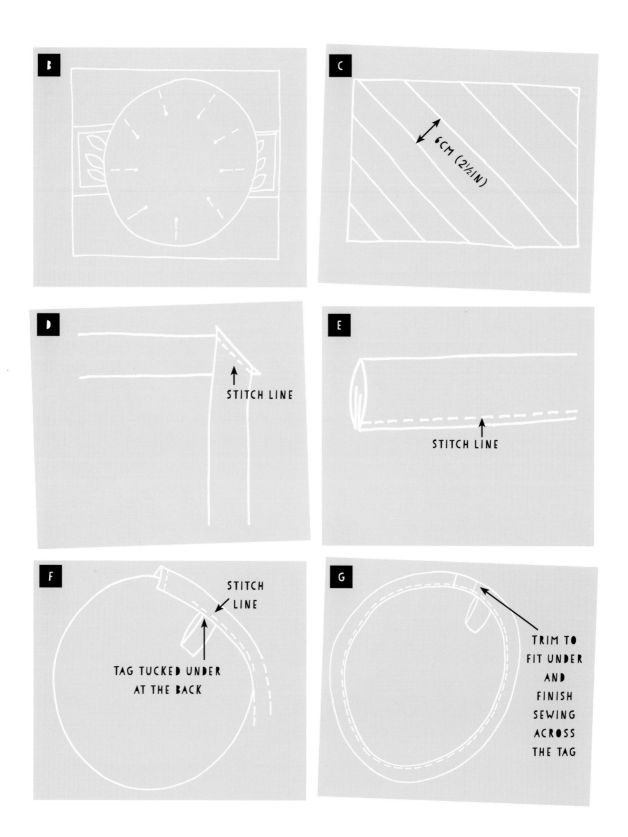

B

C
6CM (2½IN)

D
STITCH LINE

E
STITCH LINE

F
STITCH
LINE
TAG TUCKED UNDER
AT THE BACK

G
TRIM TO
FIT UNDER
AND
FINISH
SEWING
ACROSS
THE TAG

4. Photocopy and cut out the Pot Holder template and pin this to your sandwiched fabrics (B). Draw around it with a fabric pen, remove the template and cut around the drawn line. Your fabric sandwich should now be in the shape of the template.

5. To make your own bias binding, cut diagonal strips out of your binding fabric by drawing lines at 45 degrees, 6cm (2½in) apart (C). You need a total length of 50cm (20in). Cut out these strips with a rotary cutter.

6. Sew your strips together to make one long 50cm (20in) length of binding. Do this by pinning and sewing, with right sides facing,

along the diagonal, as shown below (D). Make sure the top triangle is higher up than the bottom and then sew from corner to corner.

7. Prepare your binding to sew onto the pot holder as in the Envelope Back Cushion Cover.

8. Make a hanging tag in the same way with a 5cm (2in) width of fabric. Sew along the length of the tag with a 3mm (⅛in) seam allowance (E).

9. Decide where you want the tag to be positioned – this will be your starting point. Place the binding over the edge of your pot holder and start sewing 5cm (2in) in along the binding, leaving 5cm

(2in) for finishing off. Sew as near to the open edge of the binding as you can, but do make sure your stitches are catching the binding at the back. After several stitches, tuck the tag under the binding at the back by folding it in half and placing the raw edges under the binding (F). Sew it in place as you go and continue stretching the binding around the pot holder to ensure it is smooth and flat.

10. Continue to sew all the way around and when you are almost at the beginning again trim any excess, leaving 2½cm (1in) to tuck under the beginning of the binding. Keep sewing until you have sewn across the tag again to give it a little more strength (G).

TEA COSY

SCREEN FILLER TECHNIQUE

This pretty yet functional tea cosy will bring instant style and a splash of colour to your kitchen. The bright coloured fabric printed with the fun poppy motif adds further style and humour to the project.

YOU WILL NEED:

★ Tea Cosy template (see Tea Cosy template)
★ Poppy design (see Poppy design)
★ Outer fabric, 2 pieces, 38 x 33cm (15 x 13in)
★ Lining fabric, 2 pieces, 38 x 33cm (15 x 13in)
★ Wadding (batting), 2 pieces, 33 x 28cm (13 x 11in)
★ Braid, 7½cm (3in) in length
★ Cutting mat
★ Scissors
★ Rotary cutter
★ Pins
★ Spray mount

1. Photocopy the Poppy design and prepare your screen using the screen filler method.

2. With your Poppy design, first print one or both sides of your outer fabric then allow this to dry. Once fully dry, heat set.

3. With the right sides of the fabrics facing, separately layer the two outer fabrics then the two lining fabrics. Cut out the Tea Cosy template and pin it on top of the four pieces of fabric, as shown (A).

Then carefully cut out the tea cosy shape with either scissors or the rotary cutter.

4. Once you have cut out your fabrics, pin the outer ones together with the right sides facing. Fold the braid in half and pin it in place between the two outer fabric pieces in the centre at the top, with the open edges of the braid in line with the edge of the fabric. Then sew around the curved edge approximately 19mm (¼in) from the edge (B).

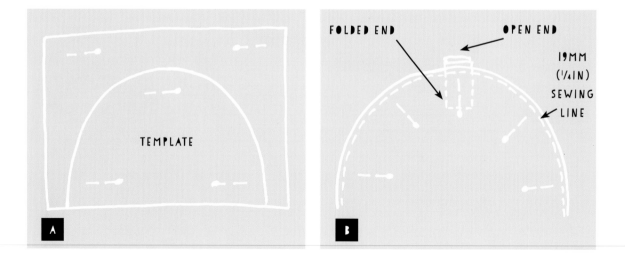

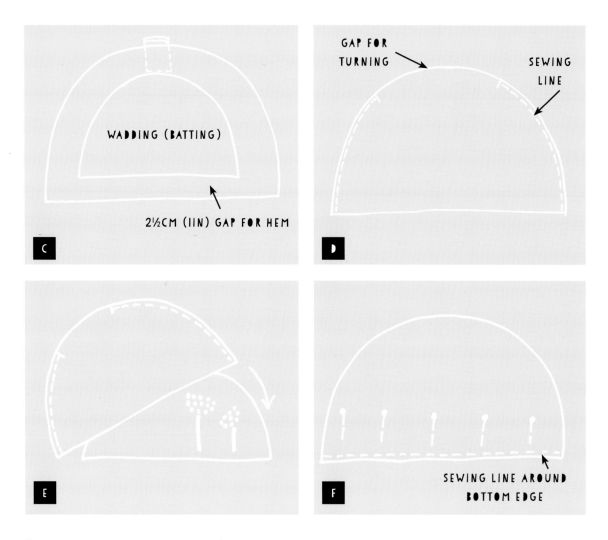

WADDING (BATTING)

2½CM (1IN) GAP FOR HEM

C

GAP FOR TURNING

SEWING LINE

D

E

SEWING LINE AROUND BOTTOM EDGE

F

5. Next layer the two pieces of wadding (batting), then pin the Tea Cosy template onto them and carefully cut them out with either scissors or the rotary cutter. In an airy room, spray mount one side of each piece of wadding (making sure to follow the manufacturer's instructions carefully when using the spray mount) and press it firmly onto each wrong side of your outer fabric cosy, leaving a 2½cm (1in) gap from the edge for the hem (C). When the spray mount has dried and the wadding is securely in place, turn your outer tea cosy fabrics and wadding the right way around.

6. Pin together the two lining pieces, right sides facing, and sew three-quarters of the way up each side as shown (D), leaving a gap at the top so you will able turn it the right way round.

7. Keeping the lining inside out, place this on top of the tea cosy so that the right sides are facing, as shown (E).

8. Pin the fabric hems together and sew all the way around the bottom of the tea cosy (F). Once you have done this, turn the cosy the right way round by pushing through the gap in the lining. Continue until you have turned the lining the right way round as well.

9. Fold under the unsewn gap in the lining and then stitch by hand to close. Finally, push the lining inside the tea cosy top, smooth it out and you are done. Now you can put the kettle on!

EGG COSY
STENCIL TECHNIQUE

Add a little brightness to your breakfast table with these sweet, colourful cosies for your boiled eggs. Simply follow the instructions for the Tea Cosy project (see Tea Cosy), using the Egg Cosy template (see Egg Cosy template) instead. Each egg cosy uses the smallest piece of fabric, so you can make up several in no time at all. These would make great little gifts, too!

YOU WILL NEED:
★ Scallop design (see Scallop design)
★ Egg Cosy template (see Egg Cosy template)
★ Outer fabric, 2 pieces, 16½ x 16½cm (6 x 6in)
★ Lining fabric, 2 pieces, 16½ x 16½cm (6 x 6in)
★ Wadding (batting), 2 pieces, 10 x 13cm (5 x 4in)
★ Braid, 7½cm (3in) in length
★ Cutting mat
★ Scissors
★ Rotary cutter
★ Pins
★ Spray mount

I. Photocopy or trace the Scallop design onto newsprint paper then cut out with a craft knife.

2. Screen print the Scallop design onto the front (and back, if you like) of your outer fabric. Allow to dry and iron on the reverse to heat set.

3. Now follow the instructions for making the Tea Cosy (see Tea Cosy), simply substituting the Egg Cosy template instead.

BISTRO APRON

STENCIL TECHNIQUE

This is a fun apron to wear when you don't need a full cover up. It provides just enough protection, and with its roomy front pocket it is useful too! I chose a sturdy denim fabric, which provides an attractive but still utilitarian feel. Its dark colour is practical and contrasts well with the fresh, white stencilled leaf.

YOU WILL NEED:

★ Large Leaf design (see Leaf design)
★ Main fabric, 81 x 43cm (32 x 17in)
★ Pocket fabric, 25½ x 39cm (10 x 15½in)
★ 2 ribbon ties, 6 x 76cm (2 x 30in)
★ Sewing machine
★ Pins

1. Photocopy or trace the Large Leaf design onto newsprint paper then cut out with a craft knife.

2. Using the stencil technique, print the Large Leaf design onto the pocket fabric and allow it to dry before heat setting.

3. To make the pocket, fold and press a 13mm (¼in) hem along the four sides of your pocket fabric; fold again along the top of the pocket to create a nicely finished edge. Sew along the top edge of the pocket; as this will be the finished edge, you might like to use one of the decorative stitches on your machine, or choose a coloured thread.

4. Fold and press the hem along all four sides of the main apron fabric. Repeat, so you have folded twice on all four sides to create a smart finish.

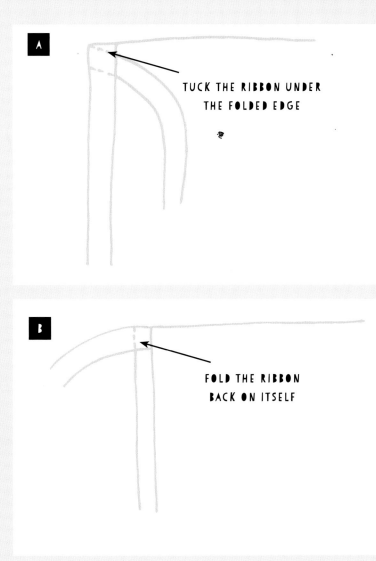

A

TUCK THE RIBBON UNDER
THE FOLDED EDGE

B

FOLD THE RIBBON
BACK ON ITSELF

5. Attach the ribbon ties to the top of the apron. To do this with your first ribbon, tuck one end of it under the folded apron edge, as shown (A).

6. Fold the ribbon back on itself, so it will be sewn with the raw edge hidden, as shown (B). Repeat the whole process with the other ribbon tie then pin both the ribbon ties in place and stitch right the way around the apron body.

7. Finally, decide where to position the pocket. Pin this in place and sew around three sides. I like to start sewing slightly above the pocket with a couple of backwards and forwards stitches to prevent it from being pulled off with time. If you'd like to split the pocket up, then sew vertical stitch lines to create compartments.

DOORSTOP

SCREEN FILLER TECHNIQUE

Even doorstops can benefit from the screen printing treatment, and are a great way to inject a little pattern and colour into a space without appearing to overwhelm it. I have designed this doorstop with a quirky wink design at the top, and used a dark, heavy duty canvas for the bottom, making it perfect for withstanding wear and tear. Choose a colour that matches the room it is peeking into, or use it to inject a spot of colour in an otherwise unused space.

YOU WILL NEED:
★ Wink design (see Wink design)
★ Handle fabric, 19 x 13cm
  (7½ x 5in)
★ Top fabric, 4 pieces, 12 x 13cm
  (5 x 4½in), 1 piece, 12 x 12cm
  (5 x 5in)
★ Canvas / denim, 4 pieces,
  12 x 7½cm (4½ x 3in), 1 piece,
  12 x 12cm (5 x 5in)
★ Filling, e.g. sand, rice, lentils
★ Wadding (batting)
★ Pins
★ Sewing machine

1. Prepare your screen with the Wink design using the screen filler method. Print your top fabric pieces and allow them to dry thoroughly.

2. Join together the four sides by pinning and sewing, with right sides facing, a screen printed piece with its dark canvas bottom piece. You should have four of these pieces sewn together, as shown (A).

3. Make a handle in the same way as for the Over-sized Beach Bag, but don't worry about finishing off the ends, as these will be sewn into the seam.

4. Using the top piece of fabric, pin both ends of the handle in place, which should leave a raised handle in the middle, as shown (B).

5. Again, like the Over-sized Beach Bag, sew from corner to corner and around all four sides to make each end secure (C).

6. Now to sew all the sides to the top of the doorstop. When you are sewing these pieces and the following ones together, start and finish 5mm (¼in) from the beginning and end of the side so you get neat corners, just like with the Bucket Bag.

7. With right sides facing, pin and sew one side to the top piece. Repeat this with all four sides so that you'd have a plus sign if you laid it out flat, as shown (D).

8. Now for sewing the adjacent sides together. Pin and sew them together, making sure the two different fabrics are level. Repeat this with the next two side panels but leave the final side unsewn.

9. To sew the base in place, with right sides facing, pin and sew along one side. Repeat this with the other three sides. You should now have all the sides sewn together apart from one of the side seams.

10. Sew the bottom two thirds of this final side, but leave the top half open to put your filling in (E).

11. Turn your doorstop the right way round and fill it up with your chosen filling. Fill up to the start of the gap and stuff the remaining space with wadding (batting).

12. Pin and hand sew the remaining length to close the gap.

ENVELOPE BACK CUSHION COVER

STENCIL TECHNIQUE

Introducing a new cushion cover or two is a great way to give a room an instant pick me up. These cushion covers with their envelope backs are quick to make, and will immediately bring new life to a room, with little effort or expense. I have chosen a retro leaf and stem design that can be printed in different colours and backed in a variety of fabrics, making it perfect for any room.

YOU WILL NEED:
★ Large Stem design (see Large Stem design)
★ Front fabric, 37 x 37cm (14½ x 14½in)
★ Back fabric, 2 pieces, 37 x 25cm (14½ x 10in)
★ Binding fabric, 2 pieces, 37 x 5cm (14½ x 2in)
★ Pillow foam / cushion inner, 38cm (15in)
★ Pins
★ Sewing machine

1. Photocopy the Large Stem design and, having folded a piece of newsprint paper lengthways, align the dotted line of the photocopied design with the folded line of the newsprint paper then cut out to make your stencil.

2. Use the stencil to print your design onto the front fabric piece. Allow it to dry thoroughly and then heat set.

3. With right side facing down, iron both bindings by folding lengthways into the middle. Next fold along the middle line so the two folded edges are folded in together then iron flat (A).

4. Pin each binding on the open edge of each piece of backing fabric then sew in place. Trim off any excess binding so the binding is the same width as the backing fabric (B).

5. To sew the cushion pieces together, position the front fabric right side up. Place the two backing pieces, overlapping in the middle, right sides down, on top of the front fabric. Make sure the binding edges are in the middle (C). Pin these layers in place and sew all around the four sides with a 1cm (½in) seam allowance.

6. To finish the edges, neatly sew around again using an over locking stitch if your machine has one, or a zigzag stitch if it doesn't.

7. Turn your cushion the right way round and insert a cushion form. Plump it up and relax!

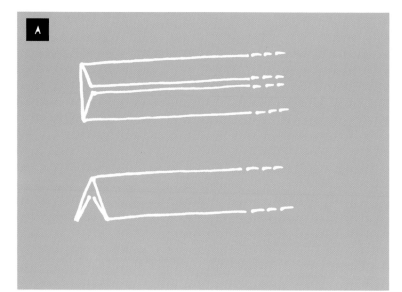

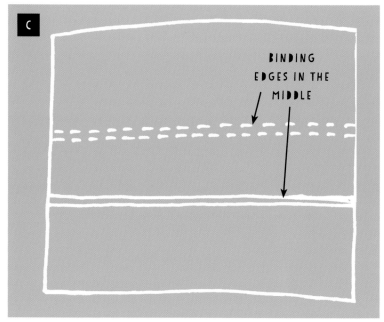

BINDING EDGES IN THE MIDDLE

NOTEBOOK COVER

STENCIL TECHNIQUE

Be warned, these are addictive! You will soon be covering everything in sight after stitching up this simple notebook cover! They also make wonderful little gifts. To make a simple design even more appealing, I have combined a panel of screen printed fabric with a coordinating fabric. Varying the coordinating fabric with the same printed panel adds further interest to a stack of books.

YOU WILL NEED:
★ Paper Doll Chain design (see Paper Doll Chain design)
★ Notebook
★ Screen printed fabric piece, the width of the opened notebook plus 2½cm (1in)
★ Outer fabric, 2 pieces, the width of the opened notebook plus 2½cm (1in)
★ Lining fabric, the size of the notebook plus 2½cm (1in) in both width and height
★ Notebook sleeves fabric, 2 pieces 15cm (6in) x height + 2½cm (1in) of notebook
★ Pins
★ Poke tool, e.g. knitting needle
★ Sewing machine

1. Fold a piece of newsprint paper concertina style to the width of your design, so you have 8 folds. Trace the Paper Doll Chain design onto the front then cut out. Position this on the underside of the screen (the smooth side), with masking tape, taping an inch above and below the paper dolls; this gives your print a nice clean edge. Also tape off the remaining unwanted area of the screen to prevent paint from seeping through.

2. Print a panel of the doll chain onto your fabric. Allow to dry thoroughly and heat set.

3. Once dry, trim this panel to size and, with right sides facing, pin and sew the top and bottom panels to it (A). Iron the seam away from the panel edge and trim this completed outer piece to the size of your lining, which should be 2½cm (1in) larger in both directions than your opened out notebook.

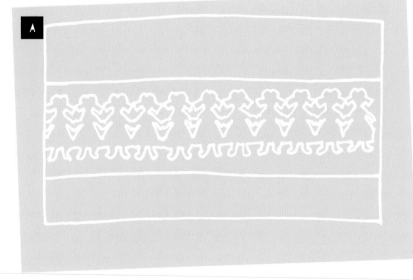

A

4. Take the outer fabric and lay this right side up. Fold each sleeve piece in half, wrong sides facing, and lay these on top of the outer fabric making sure the folded edges are innermost. Finally, place the lining fabric on top with right side down, facing the other right sides (B).

5. Pin all around and sew with a 5mm (¼in) seam, leaving a gap as shown below (C). Make sure your gap starts and finishes past the sleeves so these are sewn securely before turning.

6. Turn the cover the right way round, pushing a knitting needle into the corners to flatten them.

7. Finally, turn the seam of the open gap inwards, pin this in place and, in order to give a neat finish to your notebook, sew all the way around with a 3mm (⅛in) seam. Insert your notebook.

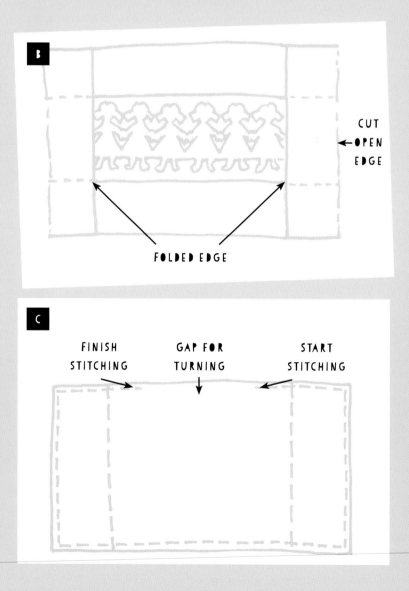

B

CUT
← OPEN
EDGE

FOLDED EDGE

C

FINISH
STITCHING

GAP FOR
TURNING

START
STITCHING

PLEATED POUCH

STENCIL TECHNIQUE

This is a pretty zipper pouch that is perfect for throwing all your essentials in and popping in your bag. The shape works really well to use as a clutch as well, to fit your keys, mobile, money and a lippy for an evening out. I have used an all over design that complements the shape of the pouch, and have found that a light, crisp fabric is suited to showing off the pleat.

YOU WILL NEED:

★ Sun Dial design (see Sun Dial design)
★ Outer fabric, 25 x 30cm (10 x 12in)
★ Lining fabric, 2 pieces, 25 x 15cm (10 x 6in)
★ Zip at least 33cm (13in)
★ Sewing machine
★ Zipper foot
★ Air dry pen
★ Pins

1. Photocopy the Sun Dial design and prepare a stencil with it on newsprint paper. Cut two lots of this design next to each other so that the stencil covers your 25 x 30cm (10 x 12in) outer fabric.

2. Print your fabric and allow to dry thoroughly before heat setting.

3. Mark the pleats on your outer fabric with your air dry pen by marking three lines at 10cm (4in), 13cm (5in) and 15cm (6in) along the shorter side. Do this on both of the shorter sides. Fold the two outer marks onto the central 13cm (5in) mark and pin in place. Sew across the pleat and repeat on the other side (A).

10CM 13CM 15CM
(4IN) (5IN) (6IN)

STITCH ACROSS
THE PLEAT ON
BOTH SIDES

A

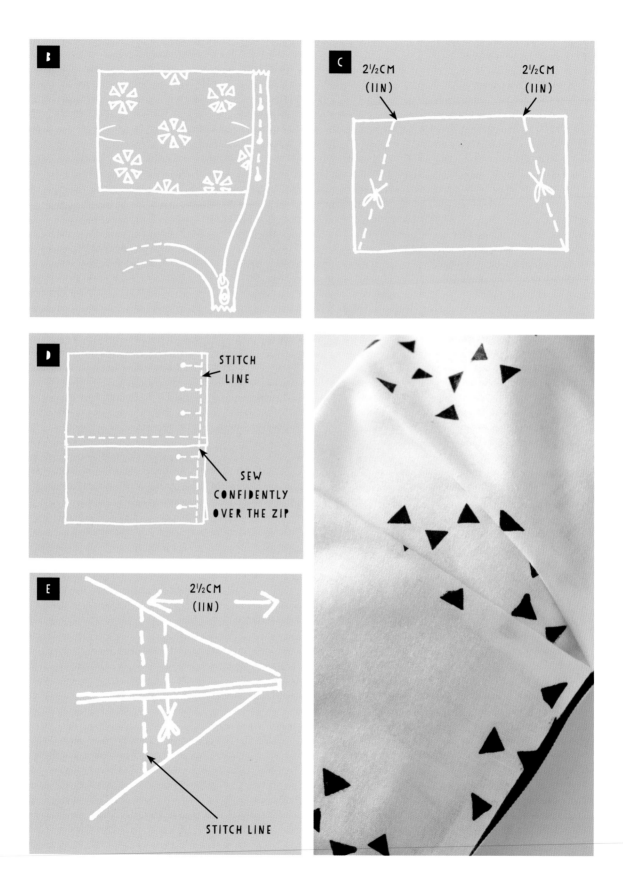

B

C
2½CM (IIN)   2½CM (IIN)

D
STITCH LINE

SEW CONFIDENTLY OVER THE ZIP

E
2½CM (IIN)

STITCH LINE

4. Attach the zipper foot to your machine. With the zipper fully open, pin the right side of the zip to the right side of the outer fabric and sew along, making sure the edge of the zipper foot is up against the teeth (B). Repeat with the other side of the zip, making sure the ends are lined up to ensure a straight zip.

5. Trim the lining to match the pouch shape by cutting from the bottom corner to 2½cm (1in) from the top edge. Do this on both sides of both lining pieces (C).

6. Pin the lining, right sides together, on top of the zip, sandwiching the zip between the two layers of fabric. Sew the lining in the same way as the outer fabric, again making sure the edge of the zipper foot is up against the teeth.

7. Important! At this point close the zip half way. If you forget, the zip fastener will be stuck outside the pouch. Trim the excess zip at the closed end at this point, too.

8. Lay out your pouch, as shown (D), with the pouch body facing upwards and the open lining facing down. Make sure the teeth on both sides of the zip are aligned and facing upwards. Pin in place and sew along this edge. Repeat with the other side of the pouch.

9. Make corners in your pouch as with the Over-Sized Beach Bag, only this time draw a line 2½cm (1in) in from the point (E).

10. Finally, turn the pouch the right way round and fold the hem of the lining inwards 5mm (¼in), or as small as you can manage. Press this in place, pin and sew as close to the edge as you can.

11. Use a pointed, blunt instrument, such as a knitting needle, to push the lining inside your pouch into the corners, and you're done!

BUCKET BAG

SCREEN FILLER TECHNIQUE

A perfect little shoulder bag for day or evening, this bag sits comfortably on the shoulder and is roomier than you might think! The magnetic clasp adds a nice touch to keep your bag secure, but it is entirely optional so you can miss out this step if you prefer. I have screen printed the Kite Strings design on one side but you could print this in any position. Due to its structured shape, I have used a stiff denim fabric but paired it with a lighter, graphic fabric to complement the printing. It would look great with a contrasting ditsy floral, too.

YOU WILL NEED:

- ★ Kite Strings design (see Kite Strings design)
- ★ Bucket Bag template (see Bucket Bag template)
- ★ Outer fabric, 2 pieces, 28 x 25cm (11 x 10in), 2 pieces, 25 x 13cm (10 x 5in), 1 piece, 28 x 13cm (11 x 5in)
- ★ Lining fabric, 2 pieces, 28 x 25cm (11 x 10in), 2 pieces, 25 x 13cm (10 x 5in), 1 piece, 28 x 13cm (11 x 5in)
- ★ Handle fabric, 84 x 15cm (33 x 6in)
- ★ Magnetic clasp (optional)
- ★ Canvas, 2 pieces, 7½ x 5cm (3 x 2in) if using magnetic clasp
- ★ Pins
- ★ Sewing machine
- ★ Spray mount

1. Photocopy the Kite Strings design and prepare your screen with the screen filler method.

2. Screen print the fabric that will be the front of the bag with the Kite Strings design, allow it to dry and heat set.

3. Cut the fabrics for the outer and the lining pieces by pinning the Bucket Bag template onto the front piece, and then the back piece of both the outer and lining pieces before cutting around (A). Using a ruler and rotary cutter, cut a line from each bottom corner to 2½cm (1in) from the top on both side panels.

A

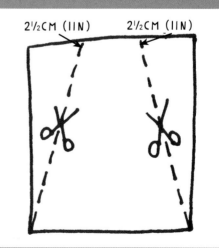

2½CM (1IN) 2½CM (1IN)

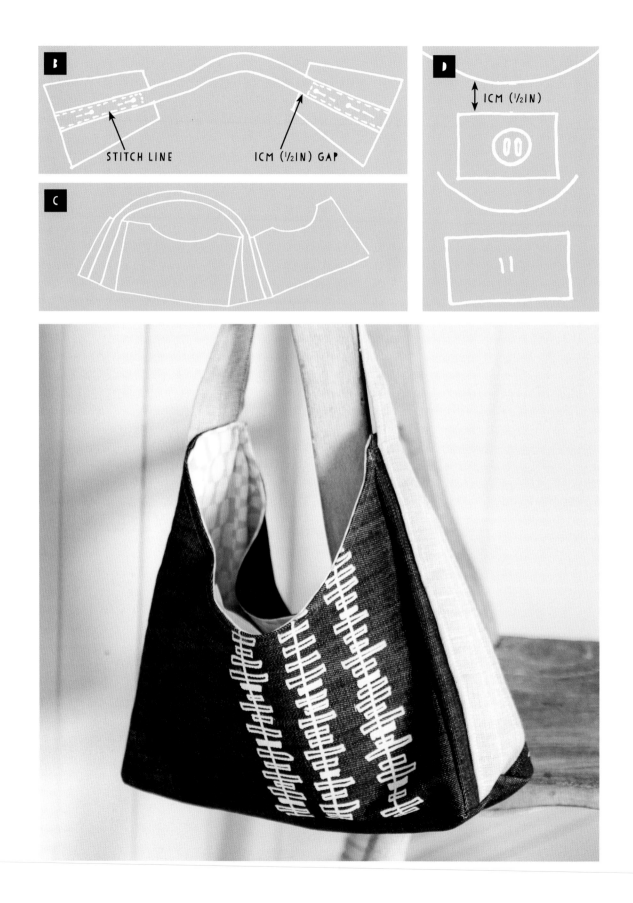

B

STITCH LINE

ICM (1/2IN) GAP

C

D

ICM (1/2IN)

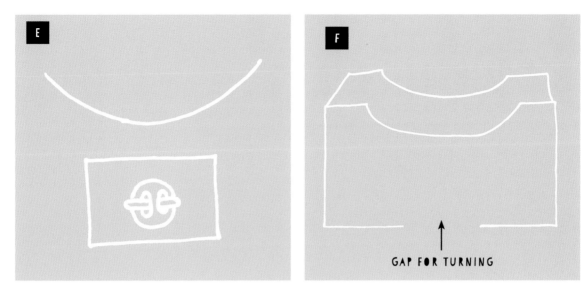

GAP FOR TURNING

4. Make the handle in the same way as the Envelope Back Cushion Cover binding, sewing along the edges and down the middle, and then pin in the middle of the side panel of the bag, as shown. Pin the other end to the other side panel and stitch in place, making sure you turn 1cm (½in) before you get to the top of the bag to leave room for when attaching the lining (B).

5. With right sides facing, sew three of the outer pieces together, leaving the fourth side free. When sewing the sides, start from the top and sew to 5mm (¼in) from the bottom, stitching backwards and forwards a couple of times to make it sturdy. You should now have a row of the four pieces (C).

6. To sew the sides to the bottom piece, start with one of the shorter sides, and with right sides facing pin in place. Beginning 5mm (¼in) down, sew to 5mm (¼in) from the bottom. Go back and forth a few times at the beginning and end to strengthen. Repeat this with all four edges and then sew the fourth open side. Next turn the right way round.

7. If you are using a magnetic clasp, now is the time to attach it to the lining. If not, go to Step 10. Spray mount your canvas pieces onto the middle of the back of the two lining pieces, 1cm (½in) down from the top to allow for the seam and turning.

8. Position one of the magnetic clasp washers in the middle of this square and mark the two rectangular slots with a pen or pencil. You won't see this mark once it is attached so use whatever shows clearly enough. Snip carefully through these two pencil lines (D).

9. From the front of the lining, push the clasp prongs through the slots; attach the washer and ease the prongs down, away from the washer. Repeat with the other side of the magnetic clasp. To ensure both are aligned I like to clasp both pieces together and then mark the slot positions (E).

10. Sew the lining pieces together in the same way as the outer fabric but leave a gap as shown in the last seam to allow for turning (F).

11. With right sides together, slip the main part of the bag into the lining, making sure the handle goes down inside the bag. Line up the seams and pin all the way around, stretching where necessary to ensure no ruching when sewing. You may need to flip the handle to the other side of the bag as you sew. Put your hand through the gap in the lining and gently move it under to the other side of the bag if it gets in the way as you are sewing.

12. When you have sewn all the way around, remove the pins, push the bag through the lining and turn it the right way.

13. Tuck in the open edge of the lining and sew this closed either by hand or machine.

14. Push the lining into the bag and iron the top edge flat so the lining lies flat inside. Sew all the way around the top of the bag with a 5mm (¼in) allowance to create a neat finish to your bag.

OVER-SIZED BEACH BAG

STENCIL TECHNIQUE

This fresh blue bag with a fun retro flower design is ideal for throwing everything in for a trip down to the beach or for a day out simply anywhere! I like to use a stronger canvas or even a waxed cotton fabric for the base of the bag and the handles to provide some sturdiness. Then I contrast this with a lighter, linen-type fabric for the top section, along with a nice crisp cotton for the lining.

YOU WILL NEED:
* Daisy Chain design
  (see Daisy Chain design)
* Top fabric, 2 pieces, 50 x 29cm
  (20 x 11½in)
* Bottom fabric, 2 pieces,
  50 x 23cm (20 x 9in)
* Lining fabric, 2 pieces,
  50 x 50cm (20 x 20in)
* Lining pocket fabric, 23 x 30cm
  (9 x 12in)
* Handle fabric, 2 pieces,
  76 x 16½cm (30 x 6½in)
* Pencil or knitting needle
* Pins
* Sewing machine

1. With the Daisy Chain design, prepare the stencil and screen as for the Notebook Cover. Print the top pieces of fabric with the Daisy Chain design then fix these to the bottom fabric pieces by pinning the right sides together and sewing with a straight stitch across the bottom. Press the front and back pieces then, with right sides still facing, sew three sides together, leaving the top open.

2. Still with the right sides facing, make corners in your bag. To do this, first push a corner out to make a triangular point, lining up the side and bottom seams on top of one another. Sew a straight line 6cm (2½in) away from the point, then trim off the corner to avoid bulk in your bag (A). Repeat with the other corner then turn your bag the right way round.

3. For the lining pocket, fold the fabric in half so the right sides are facing, then sew along two of the open sides, leaving the top open. Turn the pocket the right way round, pushing the corners out fully with a pencil or knitting needle, then fold a hem on the open side and pin. Iron the pocket then stitch across the top to create a crisp edge. Pin the pocket in the middle of one of the lining sides, about 10cm (4in) from the top of the bag, then sew in place.

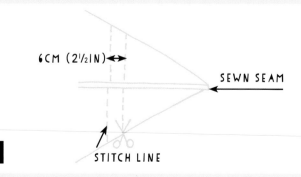

6CM (2½IN)

SEWN SEAM

A

STITCH LINE

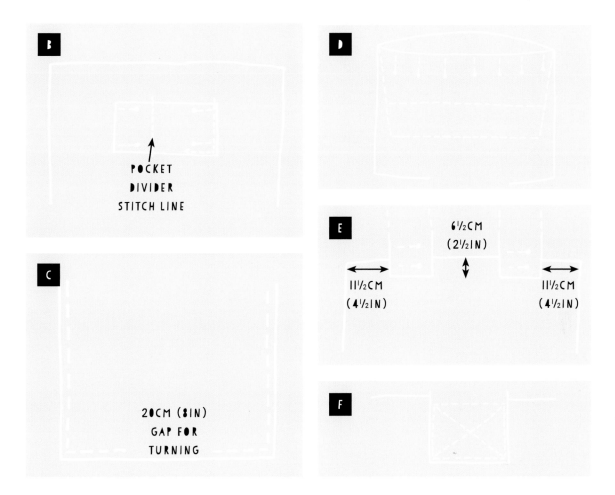

B

POCKET
DIVIDER
STITCH LINE

D

E

6½CM
(2½IN)

11½CM
(4½IN)

11½CM
(4½IN)

C

20CM (8IN)
GAP FOR
TURNING

F

4. Sew a line down the pocket as shown (B) to make a pocket divider for your phone, first checking the width of your device to establish where the line should go. You could always make a second narrow pocket at one end for a handy penholder.

5. With right sides facing, now pin around the two sides and the bottom of your lining, checking that the pocket opening is at the top. Leave a gap of approximately 20cm (8in) at the bottom as shown (C), which you will need to turn the bag the right way round. Then sew corners into the lining, as you did for the main body of the bag.

6. Now start to fix the lining in position by first placing the main part of the bag into the lining with the right sides together, lining up the seams. Pin all the way round as shown (D), stretching the fabric where necessary to ensure there is no ruching as you sew.

7. Sew all the way around the bag, then remove the pins. Push the bag through the gap in the lining to turn it the right way around, not forgetting to push the corners out, as well.

8. Tuck in then press the open edge of the lining and top stitch this closed. Push the lining into the bag and iron flat the top so that the lining lies flat inside. If you like, you can sew all the way round the

top edge of the bag with a 1½cm (½in) seam to keep the lining lying smoothly inside the bag.

9. Make a handle by following the instructions for making the cushion binding in Envelope Back Cushion Cover, except fold in the ends first to create a neat finish – these are going to show and you don't want raw edges showing. Pin each end of your handle 6½cm (2½in) down and 11½cm (4½in) in from each side, as shown (E).

10. Finally, sew your first handle in place with a crisscross and down all four sides (F) to make it nice and secure, then repeat this process with the other handle on the other side of the bag. Now you're ready for the beach!

DESK TIDIES

STENCIL TECHNIQUE

We all have bits and bobs on our desks and other work surfaces that need

to be easily accessible, so why not make a pretty container to store them in?

These little desk tidies, tall ones for pens and other utensils, and shorter, wider

ones for paper clips and the like, are perfect containers for storing everything

that would otherwise scatter in disarray.

YOU WILL NEED:
★ Scallop design (see Scallop design)
★ Pins

FOR THE WIDE DESK TIDY:
★ Wide Desk Tidy template (see Wide Desk Tidy template)
★ Denim / canvas outer fabric, 1 round piece, cut using the Wide Desk Tidy template, 1 rectangular piece, 17 x 64cm (6½ x 21½in)
★ White fabric, 1 round piece, cut using the Wide Desk Tidy template, 1 rectangular piece, 17 x 64cm (6½ x 21½in)
★ Fusible interfacing, 1cm (½in) smaller than the outer fabric pieces

FOR THE NARROW DESK TIDY:
★ Narrow Desk Tidy template (see Narrow Desk Tidy template)
★ Denim / canvas outer fabric, 1 round piece cut using the Narrow Desk Tidy template, 1 piece, 24 x 38cm (9½ x 15in)
★ White fabric, 1 round piece cut using the Narrow Desk Tidy template, 1 piece, 24 x 38cm (9½ x 15in)
★ Fusible interfacing, 1cm (½in) smaller than the outer fabric pieces

1. Photocopy two lengths of the Scallop design onto newsprint paper and cut out to make your stencil. Check that the print is the length of the fabric: 64cm (21½in) for the wide desk tidy, or 38cm (15in) for the narrow one.

2. Using the stencil technique, screen print the design onto the top half of the long white fabric, leaving 2½cm (1in) at the top for the seam. Allow this to dry thoroughly and heat set.

3. Iron the fusible interfacing onto the back of both of the denim / canvas outer fabrics.

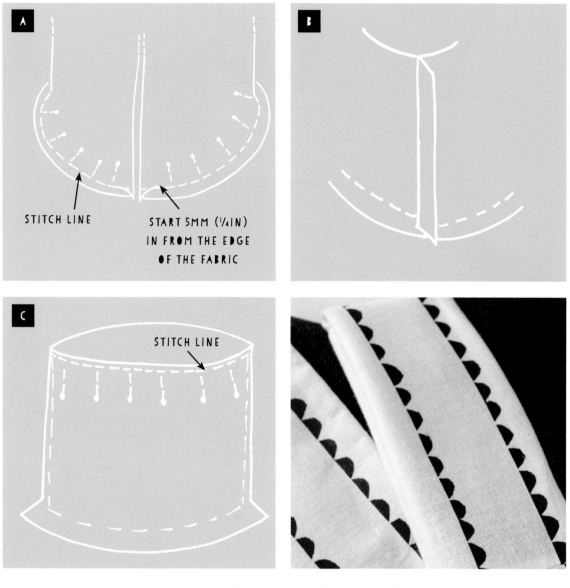

A STITCH LINE

START 5MM (¼IN)
IN FROM THE EDGE
OF THE FABRIC

B

C STITCH LINE

4. With right sides facing, pin and sew the denim / canvas rectangle onto its base, starting 5mm (¼in) in and finishing when you reach the beginning again (A). Do this slowly, as you will need to turn as you sew to stitch around the base.

5. Pin and sew the side seam to complete the outside piece of the desk tidy (B). Trim any excess fabric down the side seam with a 5mm (¼in) seam and then turn the right way round.

6. Repeat Steps 3 and 4 for the lining, but when you come to sew the side seam, start from the top and sew to half way down to leave a gap for turning.

7. Place the outer fabric inside the lining fabric so that right sides are facing. Pin and sew around the top to sew the desk tidy and lining together (C). You may need to stretch this as you pin to avoid any ruching.

8. Push the outer fabric though the lining to turn the right way round. Fold the gap seam in and hand sew to close.

9. Push the lining inside and fold over the top to the desired height. Now fill with your bits and bobs!

DESIGN TEMPLATES

SUNFLOWER

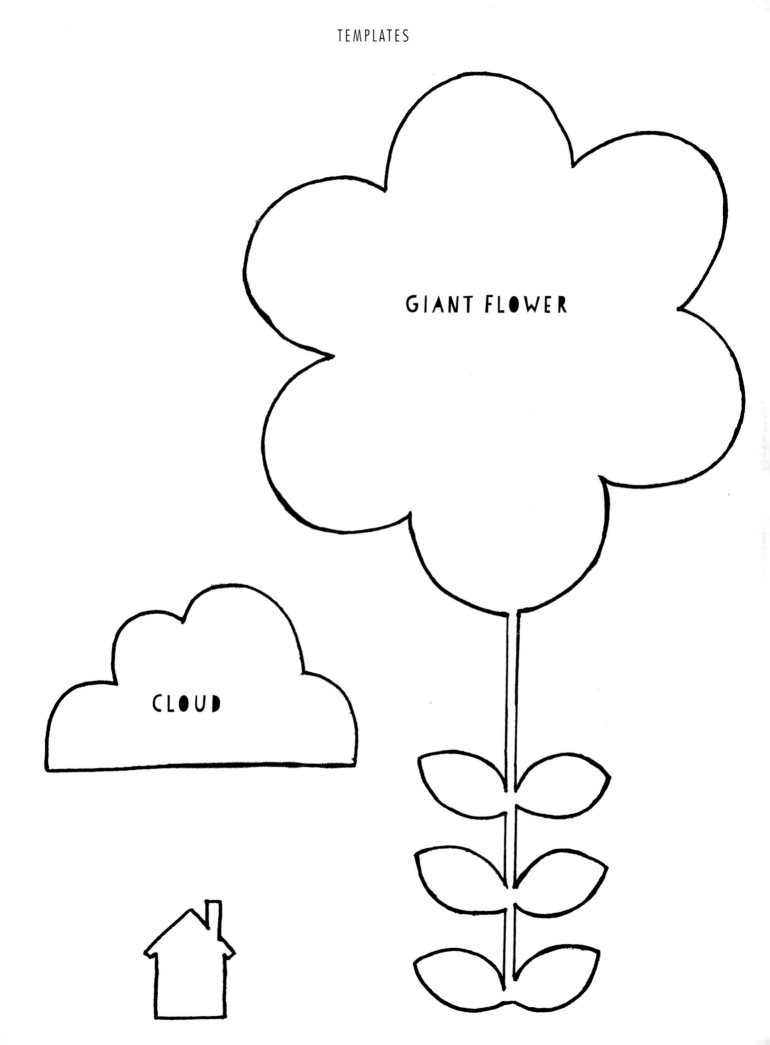

GIANT FLOWER

CLOUD

AGAPANTHUS

BUBBLES

LITTLE LEAF

POPPY

LARGE LEAF

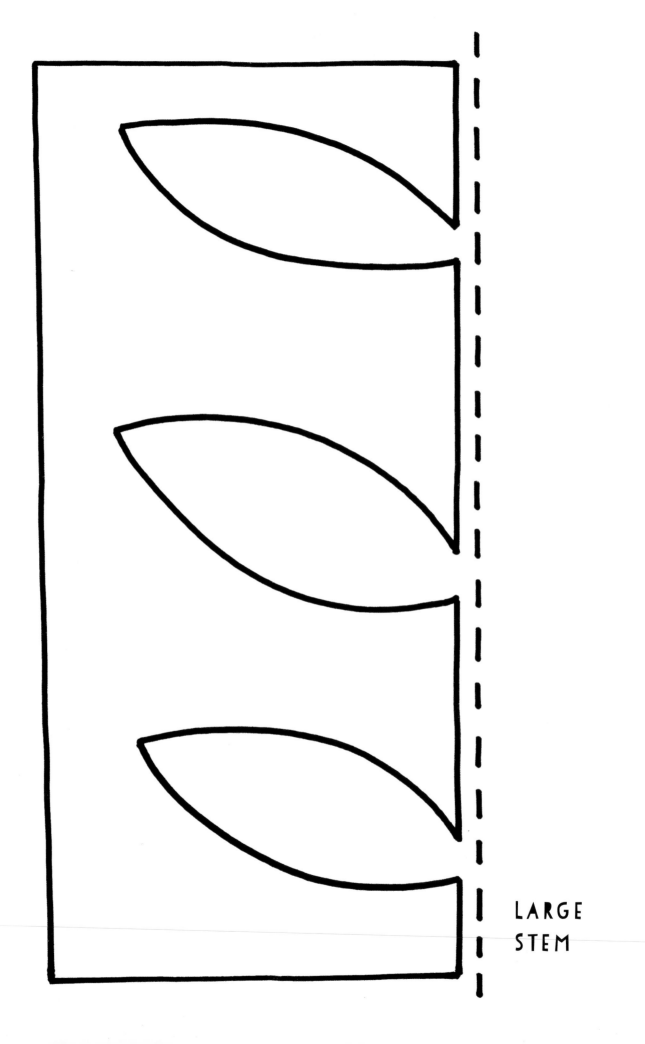

LARGE
STEM

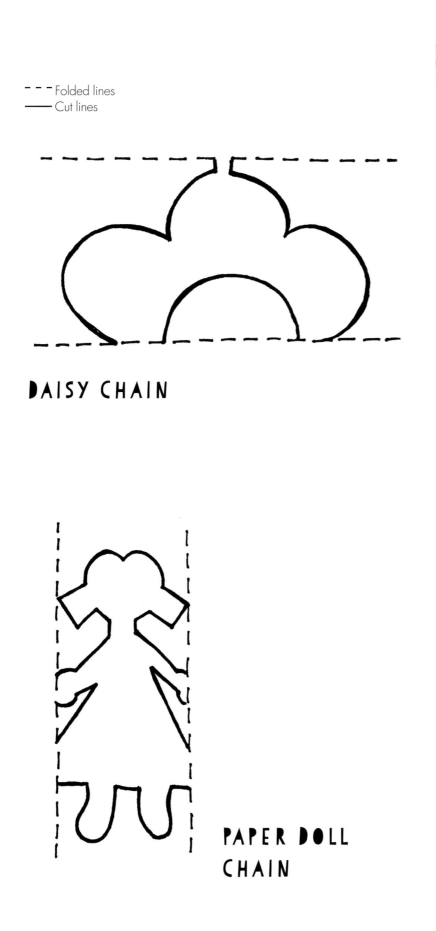

- - - Folded lines
—— Cut lines

DAISY CHAIN

PAPER DOLL
CHAIN

SCALLOP

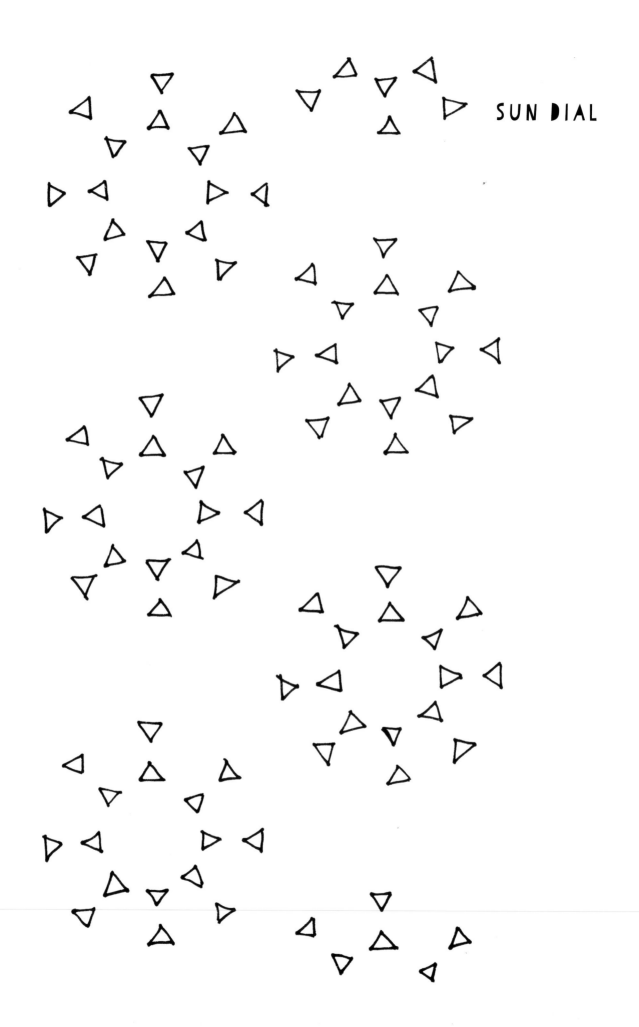

SUN DIAL

KITE STRINGS

SEWING
TEMPLATES

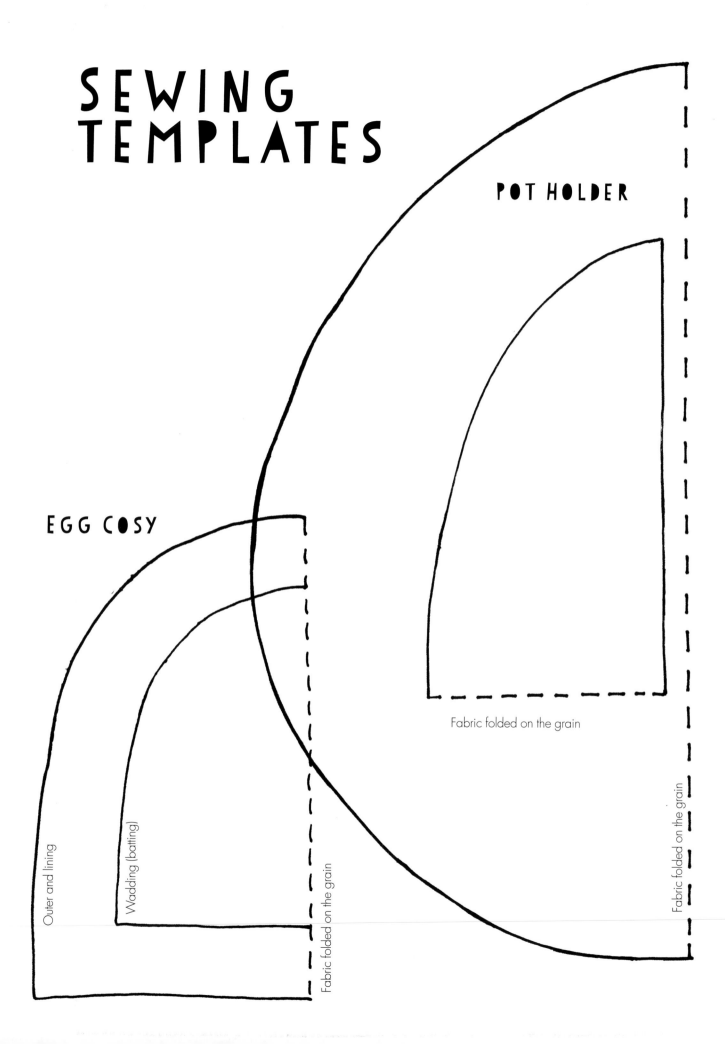

POT HOLDER

EGG COSY

Fabric folded on the grain

Outer and lining

Wadding (batting)

Fabric folded on the grain

Fabric folded on the grain

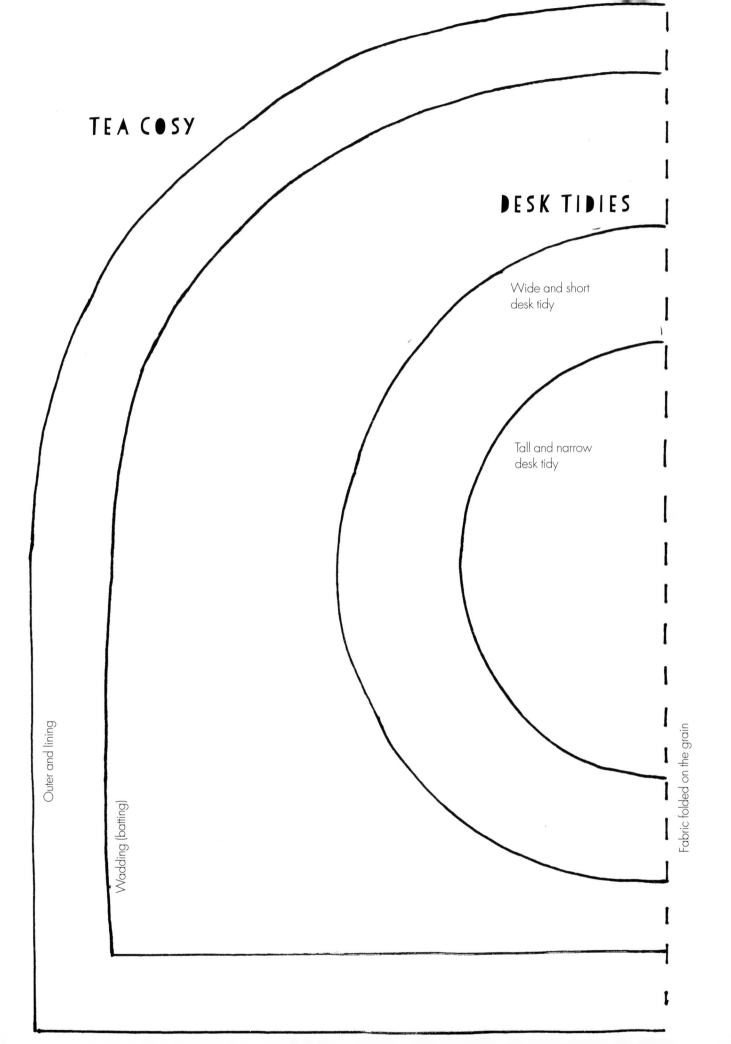

TEA COSY

DESK TIDIES

Wide and short
desk tidy

Tall and narrow
desk tidy

Outer and lining

Wadding (batting)

Fabric folded on the grain

SUPPLIERS

BACKSTITCH

Large selection of Klona solids and linen blend solids fabrics
www.backstitch.co.uk
Tel: 01480 461758
hello@backstitch.co.uk

CLOUD 9 FABRICS

Organic cotton fabrics printed with eco-responsible, low impact dyes that make beautiful fabrics to accompany sewing projects
www.cloud9fabrics.com
Tel: (908) 272 8200
info@cloud9fabrics.com

HANDPRINTED LTD

All necessary screen printing supplies including screens, squeegees, inks, textile medium, drawing fluid and screen filler
Unit 6 Horton's Yard
Melbourne Road
Chichester
West Sussex
PO19 7ND
www.handprinted.net
Tel: 01243 697606
shop@handprinted.net

HOBBYCRAFT

General craft supplies, including embroidery hoops, craft knives, cutting mats, acrylic ink and medium
www.hobbycraft.co.uk
Tel: 0330 026 1400

HOMECRAFTS DIRECT

Screen printing equipment including newsprint paper, craft knives and cutting mats
Hamilton House
Mountain Road
Leicester
LE4 9HQ
www.homecrafts.co.uk
Tel: 0116 2697733
hcenquiries@homecrafts.co.uk

MARTHA PULLEN

Great selection of fabrics, laces & trims and notions
www.marthapullen.com

M IS FOR MAKE

Large selection of plain cotton and linen fabrics, as well as lovely patterned fabrics, perfect for printing on
www.misformake.co.uk

SIMPLY SOLIDS

Large selection of plain Kona cotton fabrics amongst other great choices for printing on
www.simplysolids.co.uk

SPINSTER'S EMPORIUM

Great choice of vintage fabrics to use for your screen printing
www.spinstersemporium.co.uk
Tel: 07731 932188
hello@spinstersemporium.co.uk

STITCH CRAFT CREATE

Wide selection of sewing equipment and fabrics
www.stitchcraftcreate.co.uk

THE VILLAGE HABERDASHERY

As well as a large selection of plain and patterned fabrics to print on, The Village Haberdashery stocks other screen printing needs such as embroidery hoops and cutting mats
47 Mill Lane
London
NW6 1NB
www.thevillagehaberdashery.co.uk
Tel: 020 7794 5635
info@thevillagehaberdashery.co.uk

WHALEYS (BRADFORD) LTD

A diverse collection of fabrics in a variety of textures, including muslin and mesh, to use with embroidery hoop printing
Harris Court
Great Horton
Bradford
West Yorkshire
BD7 4EQ
www.whaleys-bradford.ltd.uk
Tel: 01274 576718
info@whaleysltd.co.uk

WICKED PRINTING STUFF

Specialist screen printing supplies including print and cut film to create a more permanent stencil
Unit 7 The Grove Workshops
Three Gates Road
Fawkham
Kent
DA3 8NZ
www.wickedprintingstuff.com
Tel: 01474 709009
sales@wickedprintingstuff.com

TO POPS, WHO AT LEAST KNEW,
AND TO MUM WHO DOES x

ABOUT THE AUTHOR

Karen Lewis is a screen printer and prolific designer-maker living in Leeds, West Yorkshire with her husband Matthew and 3 children Samuel, Noah and Ruby, who humour her passion for all things textile. Karen teaches screen printing and textiles at workshops in her home as well as in numerous galleries and craft shops in Yorkshire and beyond.

Karen's designs and textile creations can be seen in numerous magazines and websites including Love Patchwork and Quilting and Fat Quarterly. She writes a popular blog at blueberry-park.blogspot.com and her screen printed fabrics and other makes can be found in her Etsy shop at www.etsy.com/shop/blueberrypark.

ACKNOWLEDGEMENTS

First and biggest thanks go to all my immediate and extended family and friends for putting up with me during the crazy whirlwind time of writing this book… too many to mention by name but you know who you are, but particular thanks to Ruby for allowing me to use her horse design and to Stevie B for coming up trumps in the 11th hour!; to the book club girls… your advice was invaluable! Thank you to the team at D&C, including Sarah, Sarah, Matthew and Freya for their vision, enthusiasm and guidance with this book and sharing my passion for screen printing.

INDEX

A DAVID & CHARLES BOOK
© F&W Media International, Ltd 2014

David & Charles is an imprint of F&W Media International, Ltd
Brunel House, Forde Close, Newton Abbot, TQ12 4PU, UK

F&W Media International, Ltd is a subsidiary of F+W Media, Inc
10151 Carver Road, Suite #200, Blue Ash, OH 45242, USA

Text and Designs © Karen Lewis 2014
Layout and Photography © F&W Media International, Ltd 2014

First published in the UK and USA in 2014

A catalogue record for this book is available from the British Library.

ISBN-13: 978-1-4463-0409-9 paperback
ISBN-10: 1-4463-0409-4 paperback

Printed in China by RR Donnelley for:
F&W Media International, Ltd
Brunel House, Forde Close, Newton Abbot, TQ12 4PU, UK

10 9 8 7 6 5 4 3 2 1

Content Manager: Sarah Callard
Editor: Matthew Hutchings
Project Editor: Freya Dangerfield
Design Manager: Sarah Clark
Photographer: Simon Whitmore
Senior Production Controller: Kelly Smith

F+W Media publishes high quality books on a wide range of subjects.
For more great book ideas visit: www.stitchcraftcreate.co.uk